왕초보 영어회화 훈련북

왕초보 영어회화 훈련북

지은이 김수현
펴낸이 임상진
펴낸곳 (주)넥서스

초판 1쇄 인쇄 2017년 7월 10일
초판 1쇄 발행 2017년 7월 20일

출판신고 1992년 4월 3일 제311-2002-2호
10880 경기도 파주시 지목로 5
Tel (02)330-5500 Fax (02)330-5555

ISBN 979-11-6165-065-4 13740

출판사의 허락 없이 내용의 일부를
인용하거나 발췌하는 것을 금합니다.

가격은 뒤표지에 있습니다.
잘못 만들어진 책은 구입처에서 바꾸어 드립니다.

본 책은 『우선순위 영어회화 훈련북』(2015)의
개정판입니다.

www.nexusbook.com

ME-TIME BOOK
English

왕초보 영어회화 훈련북

김수현 지음

넥서스

# 머리말

영어에 익숙해지는 방법은 의외로 간단합니다.
자신의 일상을 영어로 옮겨 보는 것!

우선

1 반복되는 하루의 일과를 한글로 정리하고
2 이에 해당하는 영어 표현을 동사의 현재시제로 표현해 봅니다.

예를 들어,

나는 7시에 기상한다.
7시 50분에 집을 나선다.
8시 30분쯤 회사에 출근한다.

이를 영어로 옮기면 다음과 같습니다.(물론 이와 같거나 유사한 의미를 갖는 다른 표현들을 사용해도 좋습니다.)

I get up at 7.
I leave for work at 7:50.
I come to the office around 8:30.

반복되는 일과를 영어로 옮기는 과정이 끝나면,

3 일상생활의 특정 상황을 설정,
4 이에 필요한 표현들을 한글로 정리한 후
5 이것을 다시 영어로 옮겨 봅니다.

예를 들어,

충치가 있는 듯하다.
오늘은 반드시 치과에 간다.
오전에는 일이 바쁘다.
점심 먹고 가야지.

이를 영어로 옮기면 다음과 같이 될 것입니다.

I think I have a cavity.
I have to go to the dentist.
I'm busy this morning.
I'm going to the dentist after lunch.

이런 과정을 반복하다 보면 새로운 어휘 습득은 물론 영어 표현력이 빠르게 느는 것을 느낄 수 있습니다. 플래너에 그날 해야 할 일을 영어로 간단히 메모하는 습관 역시 영어에 익숙해지는 좋은 방법 중의 하나입니다. 스마트폰이나 컴퓨터의 언어 설정을 영어로 바꿔 사용하는 것 또한 훌륭한 방법이지요. 처음에는 대단히 불편하게 느껴지지만 몇 주 정도면 금방 익숙해질 것입니다.

〈우선순위 영어회화 훈련북〉은 이처럼 일상생활에서 반복되는 일이나 있을 법한 상황에서 필요한 표현들을 사전식으로 정리한 책입니다. 총 22개의 챕터에 인사 표현, 일상생활 표현부터 감정 표현, 학교·직장·여행지 등에서 쓰이는 표현 등을 다루고 있습니다. 늘 가까이 두고 영어로 말할 때 적극 활용해 보세요!

저자 김수현

구성과 특징

Intro

> **09 의견의 대립**
>
> 상대편과 옥신각신할 때 급기야는 "말이 안 통하는군요."라는 뜻의 You're ridiculous. 또는 You're full of nonsense. 같은 말이 나오기도 하죠. 상대편의 이해를 구하고 싶을 때는 이렇게 말해 보세요. Put yourself in my position. 바로 "입장 바꿔 놓고 생각해 보세요."입니다. 영화나 드라마에서도 자주 듣게 되는 말이죠.
>
> MP3를 들어보세요 03-U09
>
> 원어민 발음 듣기 ☑ ☐   회화 훈련 ☐ ☐   듣기 훈련 ☐ ☐

각각의 Unit은 간단한 머리말로 시작합니다. 해당 Unit의 주요 내용을 요약, 정리하여 무엇을 배워야 하는지에 대한 학습 목표를 한눈에 알 수 있습니다. 또한 그 Unit에서 알아야 할 대표적인 영어 표현, 문법에 대한 정보를 제공합니다.

Notes

> 📖 **Notes**
>
> **dreamy** (남자가) 멋있는, 근사한 **hunk** 멋진 남자 **masculine** 남자다운, 사내다운 **testosterone** 테스토스테론(남성 호르몬) **frame** 몸의 골격 **athlete** 건장한 체격의 사람 **stout** 몸이 튼튼한 **feature(s)** 이목구비, 생김새 **turn-on** 흥분시키는 것, 흥분제 **bombshell** 아주 매력적이고 섹시한 여자 **be in good shape** 몸매가 좋은 **keep in shape** 몸매를 유지하다 **curves** 여성의 곡선미 **sleek** 매끄러운, 윤기 있는

한 Unit이 끝날 때마다 〈Notes〉에 어려운 단어나 표현들을 정리하였습니다. 모르는 단어는 그냥 넘어가지 말고 바로 바로 외워 두세요. 어느샌가 어려운 표현도 척척 말하고 있는 자신을 발견하게 될 것입니다!

Expressions

약속해.	Promise me.
약속할게.	I promise you.
	I'll promise.
	You have my word.
한 가지만은 약속할 수 있어.	I can promise you one thing.
약속은 지켜야지.	You should keep promises.
약속이 있어.	I have a plan.
	I have an appointment.
	*appointment는 '병원 예약'이나 '업무 관련 약속'을 가리킬 때 주로 쓴다.

상황별 회화 표현 중에 일상생활에서 가장 많이 쓰이는 표현들을 우선 순위로 수록하였습니다. 표현 아래 ＊에는 문장에 활용할 수 있는 단어, 표현에 대한 설명 등을 추가하여 표현을 더욱 다양하고 정확하게 쓸 수 있습니다. 한글과 영어 표현을 동시에 수록하고 있어 내가 하고 싶은 말이 영어로 무엇인지 바로 알 수 있습니다.

※ 표현 아래의 ＊ 에서는 표현 속 단어의 대치어, 동의어, 반의어를 정리했습니다.

→ **대치어 표시** ex) *then → there(거기서)
= **동의어 표시** ex) *ages = years
↔ **반의어 표시** ex) *high ↔ low

회화 훈련 학습자료

3가지 학습자료들을 넥서스 홈페이지(www.nexusbook.com)에서 무료로 다운받을 수 있습니다.

듣기 훈련 MP3
미국인 성우가 normal speed로 녹음한 파일입니다. 정확한 원어민 발음을 확인해 보세요.

02-U01	1
02-U02	1
02-U03	1
02-U04	1
02-U05	1
02-U06	1
02-U07	1
02-U08	1
02-U09	1
02-U10	1

회화 훈련 MP3
원어민 음성을 듣고 따라 말해 볼 수 있도록 구성했습니다. 음성은 두 번 들려 줍니다. 두 번씩 따라 말해 보고 회화 훈련 □□ 에 ✓ 표시를 하세요. 회화 표현이 입에 붙을 때까지 반복해서 말하는 연습을 하세요.

쓰기 훈련 워크북
문제를 풀면서 책에서 공부한 내용을 확인해 보세요. 다양한 유형의 문제풀이를 통해 배운 내용을 복습할 수 있습니다. 틀린 문제는 꼭 책에서 내용을 다시 한번 확인하세요.

이 책의 100% 활용법

Step 1
주제·상황별 회화 표현 확인하기

주제별, 상황별로 분류한 왕초보 필수 회화 표현들을 담았습니다. 먼저 눈으로 표현을 익히고 읽어 보세요. '듣기 훈련 MP3'를 들으며 정확한 발음을 확인하세요.

Step 2
회화 훈련

입에서 자연스럽게 영어회화가 나오도록 하려면 말하는 연습을 반복해서 해야겠죠? '회화 훈련 MP3'를 듣고 의미를 생각하면서 말하는 훈련을 합니다. 귀로 듣고 바로 입으로 따라 하는 것이 포인트! MP3를 들었을 때 의미가 잘 생각이 안 난다면, 책에서 오른쪽에 나오는 영어 표현을 손으로 가리고 왼쪽의 한글 뜻을 보면서 MP3를 들어 보세요. 한 문장당 세 번 이상 말하는 연습을 합니다.

Step 3
쓰기 훈련

'쓰기 훈련 워크북'에는 다양한 유형의 복습 문제들이 있습니다. 문제를 풀면서 책에서 공부한 내용을 다시 한번 복습하고 실력을 확인해 보세요. 입으로 말하기 연습을 하는 것도 중요하지만, 손으로 쓰는 과정을 거치면 기억에 더 오래 남습니다.

목차

Chapter 01
인사 표현(Greeting)

01	첫 만남, 인사하기	16
02	안부 묻고 대답하기	18
03	날씨와 계절 관련 표현	20
04	친구 소개하기, 소개 받기	22
05	작별하기	24

Chapter 02
대화하기(Conversation)

01	대화를 시작할 때	28
02	대화를 진행하면서	29
03	맞장구치기	30
04	간섭, 끼어들기	32
05	오해 풀기, 사과하기	34
06	말다툼	36
07	비밀에 대해 말하기	38
08	뉴스(소식) 전하기	40
09	농담하기	41
10	뒷담화	43

Chapter 03
의견(Opinion)

01	의견 제시하기	46
02	확신과 결심에 대한 표현	47
03	질문과 대답	49
04	찬성과 반대	51
05	설득하기	53
06	제안의 수락과 거절	54

Chapter 04
감정 표현(Emotion)

01	기쁨, 즐거움, 감동	58
02	슬픔	60
03	우울함, 외로움	62
04	낙담, 후회	64
05	위로, 격려	66
06	불쾌함, 화남	68
07	(상대방에 대한) 비난	70
08	(자신에 대한) 불평, 불만	72
09	싸움	73
10	긴장, 초조	74
11	두려움, 놀람	75
12	창피, 당황스러움	77
13	귀찮음, 성가심	78
14	그리움	80

15 걱정, 근심	81	
16 의심	82	

Chapter 05
대인 관계(Relationship)

01 감사 표현	84
02 축하, 축복	85
03 칭찬하기	86
04 양해와 부탁	88
05 사과와 용서	89
06 약속	91
07 손님 초대	93
08 절친함	94
09 냉대, 무시	95
10 반어적, 빈정거리는 표현	96

Chapter 06
외모(Appearance)

01 잘생김, 예쁨	98
02 못생김	101
03 개성, 분위기	103
04 성형 수술	105
05 차림새	106

Chapter 07
성격(Personality)

01 개혁적인 성격	110
02 다정다감한 성격	111
03 성공 지향적인 성격	112
04 낭만적인 성격	113
05 지적인 타입	114
06 성실, 안정적인 성격	115
07 열정적인 성격	116
08 솔직하고 과감한 성격	117
09 외유내강인 성격	118
10 기타	119

Chapter 08
사랑(Love)

01 소개팅에서	122
02 신상 파악하기	124
03 데이트 신청하기	126
04 사랑 고백	127
05 수락과 거절	129
06 연애 초기	130
07 연애 중	132
08 프러포즈	134
09 결혼 생활	135
10 이별할 때	137

Chapter 09
하루 일과(Daily routine)

01 평일 오전	140
02 평일 오후, 저녁	142
03 주말	143
04 명절, 국경일, 기념일	146

Chapter 10
학교(School)

01 대학 지원하기	148
02 수강 신청 하기	150
03 강의실에서	151
04 과제물, 시험 준비	153
05 성적	155

Chapter 11
직장(Workplace)

01 구직 활동	158
02 면접 보기	160
03 첫 출근	162
04 회의 및 보고	164
05 식사, 휴식시간	166
06 지각, 결근, 휴가	167
07 거래처 방문, 손님 접대	169
08 출장	170

Chapter 12
음식(Food)

01 좋아하는 음식	172
02 식사 주문하기	173
03 술자리에서	175
04 식당 평가	177
05 계산하기	178

Chapter 13
쇼핑(Shopping)

01 매장에서	180
02 상품 비교, 선택하기	182
03 가격 흥정하기	184
04 계산, 포장하기	185
05 교환, 환불하기	186

Chapter 14
교통(Transportation)

01 교통수단　　　　　　　188
02 교통 상황　　　　　　　189
03 지하철과 버스 타기　　190
04 택시 타기　　　　　　　192
05 대중교통 티켓 요금　　194
06 면허 따기, 운전하기　　195
07 주유, 세차하기　　　　197
08 교통 법규　　　　　　　198

Chapter 15
전화(Telephone)

01 전화 받기, 바꿔 주기　　200
02 전화 걸기, 전화 끊기　　202
03 메모 받기, 메모 남기기　204
04 용건 묻고 말하기　　　　206
05 전화 상태, 통화 시 상황　207

Chapter 01

인사 표현
Greeting

01 첫 만남, 인사하기 **02** 안부 묻고 대답하기 **03** 날씨와 계절 관련 표현
04 친구 소개하기, 소개 받기 **05** 작별하기

첫 만남, 인사하기

첫 만남과 재회, 우연한 만남 등에 따라 사용하는 표현들이 조금씩 다르니 구분해서 알아두어야 합니다. 특히 오랜만에 만났을 때는 '그동안 계속 못 만나 왔다'는 의미에서 have[has]+과거분사[현재완료]를 사용해야 하는 것도 잊지 마세요.

원어민 발음 듣기 ☑□　회화 훈련 □□　듣기 훈련 □□

□ 안녕하세요(안녕)!

Hello! / Hi!
Hi, there!
Good morning!
*Good afternoon! 점심 인사 / Good evening! 저녁 인사

□ 처음 뵙겠습니다.

How do you do?

□ (좋은) 말씀 많이 들었어요.

I heard so many (great) things about you.

□ 만나서 반갑습니다.

(It's) Nice to see you.
*nice=great, happy, glad

□ 이게 누구야!

Look who is here!

□ 오랜만이야.

Long time no see.
It has been a long time.
It has been a while.
You're quite a stranger.
I haven't seen you in ages.
*ages=years, centuries

□ 다시 만나 반가워.

It's nice to see you again.
Great to see you again.
I'm so glad to see you again.
*glad=happy, excited

□ 세상 좁다!	(What a) Small world!
□ 그동안 어디 있었어?	Where have you been?
	Where have you been hiding?
□ 지방에 있었어.	I was out of town.
□ 외국에 있었어.	I was in another country.
□ (회사 일로) 그동안 바빴어.	I have been busy (doing work).
□ 우리 만난 적 있나요?	Have we met before?
	Haven't we met before?
	I think we have met (before).
□ 파티에서 만난 것 같아요.	I think we have met at the party.
□ 제가 아는 분 같은데.	Do I know you?
	I think I know you.
□ 저를 아세요?	Do you know me?
□ 낯이 익네요.	You look familiar to me.
□ 저를 기억하세요?	(Do you) Remember me?
□ 혹시 Ms. Kim 아니세요?	Aren't you Ms. Kim?
	Aren't you Ms. Kim by any chance?
	You are Ms. Kim, right?
□ 다른 사람과 착각했어요.	I thought you were someone else.
	I took you for someone else.

📄 Notes

stranger 낯선 사람, 오랜만에 만나는 사람   hide 숨다, 숨어 지내다   look familiar to ~에게 낯익다   by any chance 혹시, 우연히   I thought ~ ~인 줄 알았다   take A for B A를 B로 착각하다(잘못 보다)

02 안부 묻고 대답하기

MP3를 들어보세요 01-U02

서양에서도 서로의 안부를 묻는 것은 인간관계를 돈독히 하는 데 중요한 역할을 합니다. How are you?, How are you doing? 같은 안부를 묻는 질문과 I'm great.(잘 지내.), So-so.(그저 그래.) 같은 적절한 답변을 잘 알아두면 문화가 다른 외국인과도 깊은 교감을 나눌 수 있습니다.

원어민 발음 듣기 ☑☐ 회화 훈련 ☐☐ 듣기 훈련 ☐☐

□ 어떻게 지냈어?

How are you?
How are you doing?
How is it going?
How is everything with you?
What's up?
What's new?
Anything new?

□ 잘 지내.

I'm great.
*I'm great. = I'm good. / I'm fine.

Everything is going well.
Couldn't be better.

□ 그저 그렇지 뭐.

So-so.
Not much.
Nothing special.

□ 잘 지내지 못해.

Not so good.

□ 항상 똑같지 뭐.

Same as always.
*always = usual

About the same.

□ 그동안 어떻게 지냈어?

How have you been?
How have you been doing?

	What have you been up to?
□ 잘 지냈어.	I have been great.
□ 잘 지내지 못했어.	I haven't been well.
□ 가족은 어때?	How is your family?
□ 다들 잘 지내.	They are all good.
□ 하는 일은 어때?	How is your work? *work = business
□ 학교생활은 어때?	How is your school?
□ 잘 되고 있어.	It is great.
□ 늘 바쁘게 지내.	I'm always busy. (I'm) Busy as always. I keep myself busy.
□ 좋아 보인다.	You look great! *great = wonderful, fantastic
□ 안색이 별로다.	You don't look so good.
□ 점점 젊어지네.	You're getting younger.
□ 살 빠졌니?	Have you lost your weight?
□ 전혀. 오히려 요즘 쪘는걸.	Not at all. I put on some weight lately.
□ 요즘 운동하니?	Have you been working out?

Notes

get+비교급 점점 ~해지다   **lose weight** 체중이 감소하다, 살 빠지다   **put on weight** 체중이 늘다, 살찌다(= gain weight)   **work out** 운동하다

03 날씨와 계절 관련 표현

MP3를 들어보세요 01-U03

외국인과 간단한 인사를 나눈 후 딱히 할 말이 없어 분위기가 어색해지는 때가 있었나요? 그럴 때는 It's a nice day, right?, It's freezing cold. 등과 같은 날씨나 계절 얘기를 해 보세요. 식상한 듯하지만 공감대를 이끌어내는 데는 최고입니다. 날씨나 계절을 말할 때는 가짜 주어 "it"을 사용하는 것도 꼭 기억하세요.

원어민 발음 듣기 ☑☐　　회화 훈련 ☐☐　　듣기 훈련 ☐☐

□ 날씨 어때?
How is the weather?
What is the weather like?

□ 오늘 날씨 좋다.
It's a nice day today.
*nice = great, fine, pleasant
The weather is great today.
What a lovely day today!

□ (오늘) 날씨 안 좋아.
The weather is bad today.
The weather sucks.

□ 비가 오려나.
It looks like rain.
It's likely to rain.

□ 태풍이 오고 있어.
The typhoon is coming.
The storm is on the way.

□ 비가 내리고 있어.
It is raining.

□ 바람이 불고 있어.
It is windy.

□ 안개가 꼈어.
It is foggy.

□ 날씨가 너무 덥고 습해.
It is really hot and humid.
It is really muggy.

□ 날씨가 너무 추워.
It is freezing cold.

□ 길이 꽁꽁 얼어서 미끄러워.
The roads are frozen and icy.

□ 내일 날씨 어때?	How will the weather be tomorrow? What will the weather be like tomorrow?
□ 일기예보에 따르면 ~	The weather forecast says… According to the weather forecast…
□ 내일 흐릴 거래.	It will be cloudy tomorrow.
□ 내일 32℃까지 올라간대.	The temperature will go up to 32℃(degrees) tomorrow.
□ 내일 비가 올 확률이 70%래.	There is a 70% chance of showers tomorrow.
□ 이제 곧 봄이야.	Spring is just around the corner. *summer 여름 / autumn 가을 / winter 겨울
□ 완연한 봄이네.	Spring is already here. Spring has clearly set in.
□ 곧 장마가 시작돼.	The rainy season is coming soon. The rainy season will start soon.
□ 나뭇잎이 붉게 물들었어.	The leaves are changing colors.
□ 요즘 일교차가 심해.	There is a big temperature gap these days.
□ 오늘 첫눈이 올 거래.	There will be the first snowfall today. We will see the first snow today.
□ 올 겨울은 눈이 많이 오네.	We have a lot of snow this winter.

Notes

suck 빨다, 아주 불쾌하다   muggy 찌는 듯이 무더운(=hot and humid)   shower 소나기
set in ~ 계절이 시작되다, 자리 잡다   snowfall 눈 내림, 강설량

04 친구 소개하기, 소개 받기

서로가 자신을 소개하거나 제삼자를 소개할 때는 동사 introduce(소개하다)와 This is ~.(이쪽은 ~입니다.)가 핵심적인 표현입니다. 처음 만나면 소개말과 함께 남녀노소 상관없이 악수를 나누는 것(shaking hands)이 보편적입니다.

□ 크리스털, 이쪽은 수야.	Crystal, this is Sue.
□ 제 친구 크리스털을 소개할게요.	I would like to introduce a friend of mine, Crystal.
	Let me introduce my friend, Crystal.
	I want you to meet my friend, Crystal.
	Everyone, this is my friend, Crystal.
	Everyone, meet my friend, Crystal.
□ 제 소개를 할게요.	Let me introduce myself.
	Let me tell you about myself.
	Allow me to introduce myself.
□ 꼭 한번 뵙고 싶었어요.	I have always wanted to meet you.
	I was looking forward to meeting you.
	We finally meet.
□ 정식으로 인사한 적은 없네요.	I don't think we have been introduced formally.
□ 뵙게 되어 영광입니다.	It is a great honor to meet you.
□ 우리 친하게 지내요.	I hope we get to know each other better.
□ 성함을 여쭤봐도 될까요?	What's your name?
	Can I have your name?
	*Could I ~?나 May I ~?는 공손한 표현이다.

☐ 당신을 뭐라고 불러야 할까요?	What should I call you? How should I address you?
☐ 그냥 '수'라고 불러 주세요.	Just call me Sue. Sue is fine.
☐ 어떤 일을 하세요?	What do you do (for a living)? What is your profession? What business are you in?
☐ 연락처를 알려 주시겠어요?	Can I have your contact info? I would like to have your contact number.
☐ 제 명함입니다.	Here is my (name) card. This is my business card. Let me give you my card.
☐ 이 번호로 연락하시면 됩니다.	You can reach me at this number.
☐ 언제든지 연락 주세요.	Call me anytime.
☐ 근처에 오시면 들르세요.	When you are in the neighborhood, please stop by.
☐ 언제든 환영입니다.	You are always welcome.
☐ 그를 소개시켜 주실 수 있나요?	Could you introduce me to him, please? If it is not too much trouble, please introduce me to him.
☐ 언제 점심 식사 함께해요.	Let's have lunch together sometime.

📝 Notes

get to know 알게 되다   address 주소, 호칭, ~라고 부르다   profession 직업, 전문직
reach 닿다, 연락을 취하다   stop by 잠깐 들르다   sometime 나중에 언제

05 작별하기

MP3를 들어보세요 01-U05

사람 사이의 헤어짐은 돌아서면 그만이라고 생각하기 쉽지만 결코 그렇지 않습니다. Good bye.(잘 가.)라는 말과 함께 It was really fun.(정말 즐거웠어.), See you again.(다음에 또 보자.)라고 하거나, 참석하지 못한 사람에 대해서는 Say hello to ~.(~에게 안부 전해 줘.)라고 할 수 있겠죠.

원어민 발음 듣기 ☑☐   회화 훈련 ☐☐   듣기 훈련 ☐☐

☐ 안녕히 가세요(계세요).
(Good) Bye.
Bye-bye.
Later.
Take care.
So long.
Farewell.

☐ 좋은 하루 되세요.
(Have a) Good day.

☐ 이제 가야겠다.
I think I should go.
I'm afraid I have to go.
I have got to go.

☐ 이제 그만 갈까?
Are you ready to go?

☐ 오늘 만나서 반가웠어요.
It was nice meeting you.

☐ 이야기 나눠서 좋았어요.
It was great talking to you.

☐ 오늘 정말 즐거웠어요.
I had a really great time today.
It was really fun.
It has been a real pleasure.

☐ 조만간 또 만나요.
See you again.
*again = soon, later, around

Let's meet real soon.
Let's do this again.

☐ 오늘 초대해 주셔서 감사해요.	Thank you for inviting me. Thank you for having me.
☐ 오늘 와 주셔서 감사해요.	Thank you for coming. I appreciate your coming. I'm glad you came.
☐ 우리 연락하며 지내요.	Let's keep in touch. Stay in touch.
☐ 전화할게.	I will call you.
☐ 이메일 할게.	I will e-mail you.
☐ 우리 나중에 더 이야기해요.	Let's talk more later.
☐ 시간 될 때 놀러 오세요.	Come by when you are available. Visit us time to time.
☐ 가족에게 안부 전해 주세요.	Say hello to your family. Give my regards to your folks. *regards = best, love
☐ 운전 조심해.	Drive safely.
☐ 집에 도착하면 문자 줘.	Text me when you get home.

📝 Notes

I'm afraid ~ 안타깝게도 ~하다, ~해서 안타깝다   appreciate 고맙게 생각하다, 감사하다
available 이용 가능한, 여유가 있는   regards 안부(=best)   folks 가족, 친지들   get home
집에 다다르다, 도착하다

Chapter 02
대화하기
Conversation

01 대화를 시작할 때   02 대화를 진행하면서   03 맞장구치기   04 간섭, 끼어들기
05 오해 풀기, 사과하기   06 말다툼   07 비밀에 대해 말하기   08 뉴스(소식) 전하기
09 농담하기   10 뒷담화

대화를 시작할 때

MP3를 들어보세요 02-U01

단도직입적으로 본론부터 말하기보다는 "있잖아.", "들어 봐." 등의 가벼운 표현으로 말을 시작하면 대화를 훨씬 부드럽게 이끌어갈 수 있습니다. 또는 Do you know ~?(~을 알아?)나 Guess ~.(~을 맞춰 봐.) 등 상대방의 관심을 끌 수 있는 표현들을 넌지시 던지는 것도 좋은 방법이죠.

원어민 발음 듣기 ☑☐   회화 훈련 ☐☐   듣기 훈련 ☐☐

☐ 있잖아.
You know what?
Guess what?

☐ 들어 봐.
Listen (to me).
I will tell you what.

☐ 안 들으면 후회할걸.
You've got to hear this.
You don't want to miss this.

☐ 어제 무슨 일 있었는지 알아?
Do you know what happened yesterday?

☐ 어디서부터 시작해야 하나?
Where do I (even) begin?
I don't know where to begin.

☐ 할 말이 있는데…….
I have something to tell you.
Can we talk now?

☐ 우리 얘기 좀 해.
We need to talk.
Let's go someplace to talk.

☐ 잠깐 시간 있어?
Do you have a minute?
Got a second?

 Notes

have got to ~해야만 하다   miss 놓치다, 그리워하다   minute 아주 잠깐의 시간(= second)
chat 잡담하다, 수다 떨다

02 대화를 진행하면서

대화를 이끌어갈 때는 eye contact(눈 맞춤)와 함께 상대방이 자신의 말을 잘 듣고 있는지 확인할 필요가 있습니다. 반대로 듣는 사람은 말하는 사람의 말을 경청하고 있다는 표현과 더불어 좀 더 이야기해 달라는 관심의 표현을 곁들일 수 있겠죠.

원어민 발음 듣기 ☑☐　회화 훈련 ☐☐　듣기 훈련 ☐☐

□ 계속해.
Please continue.
Go on.
Keep going.
Keep talking.

□ 그래서 어떻게 됐어?
Then what?
What happened next?

□ 듣고 있어.
I'm listening.
I'm paying attention to you.
I'm all ears.

□ 내 말 듣고 있어?
Are you listening to me?
Are you with me?
Are you following me?

□ 어디까지 이야기했더라?
Where am I?
Where are we?

□ 좀 더 이야기해 봐.
Tell me more.

□ 좀 더 자세히 이야기해 봐!
Details! Details!

📝 Notes

go on 계속하다　keep -ing 계속 ~하다　go ahead 어서 해, 먼저 해　be all ears 귀 기울이다, 잘 듣다　be with ~ ~와 함께하다, 잘 듣다　details 자세한 내용, 세부사항

03 맞장구치기

네이티브들은 대화 중간중간에 적절히 맞장구를 치는데 언어 습관이 다른 우리에겐 생소하게 느껴질 수 있습니다. "그래(요)?"라고 할 때는 Oh? 또는 Is that so?라고 하고, "맞아(요)."는 That's right.나 Exactly., 그리고 "설마 그럴 리가(요)."라고 할 땐 No way!나 You're kidding, right?라고 하면 됩니다.

원어민 발음 듣기 ☑☐ 회화 훈련 ☐☐ 듣기 훈련 ☐☐

☐ 그래요?

Is that so?
Is that right?

☐ 그래서요?

So?
And?

☐ 어쩌라고요?

So what?
I hear you.

☐ 정말이요?

Really?
You don't say.
(Are) You serious?

☐ 아마도. / 글쎄.

Well!
Maybe!
Probably.
I'm afraid so.

☐ 맞아요. / 그러게요.

That's right.
Exactly.
You bet.
I know.
Tell me about it.

☐ 내 말이!

That's exactly what I'm saying.
You read my mind.

☐ 설마 그럴 리가요.	No way! You're kidding, right? I can't believe it. Impossible!
☐ 그럼요. / 물론이죠.	That's true. Of course. Yes, indeed. I agree. I think so.
☐ 그래서 그랬군요.	That's why.
☐ 그렇게 된 것이구나.	That's what really happened.
☐ 말이 되네.	That explains a lot.
☐ 말도 안 돼요.	That is ridiculous. Nonsense!
☐ 너무하네요.	That is too much. That is crazy. That went too far.
☐ 잘 됐어요.	Good for you! How nice! That is so great.
☐ 안됐네요.	I'm sorry (to hear that). That's too bad. What a shame!

Notes

read one's mind 마음을 읽다, 마음이 통하다   take the word right out of one's mouth ~가 하고 싶은 말을 바로 이해하다   indeed 물론, 정말로   ridiculous 터무니없는   go far 멀리 가다, 지나치다   shame 유감, 면목 없음

04 간섭, 끼어들기

도중에 상대방의 말을 끊을 때는 간단히 Wait! 또는 Hold it right there!라고 하면 됩니다. 상대방의 말이 이해가 잘 안 될 때는 "뭐라고요?"라는 의미로 Sorry? 또는 Excuse me?라고 하죠. 또한 "나 아직 말 안 끝났어요."라고 할 땐 I'm not done yet. 또는 I'm not finished.라고 합니다.

원어민 발음 듣기 ☑☐   회화 훈련 ☐☐   듣기 훈련 ☐☐

□ 잠깐! / 그만!
Wait!
Hold it right there!
Excuse me one second.

□ 무슨 말을 하려는 거야?
What are you saying?
What are you telling me?
What are you trying to say?
What are you getting at?

□ 무슨 말 하려는지 알겠어.
I think I know what you're saying.
I think I know what you are getting at.

□ 무슨 뜻이야?
What do you mean?
What are you suggesting?

□ 무슨 말인지 통 모르겠어.
I don't understand.
I don't understand a single word.
I don't get it.
I'm not following.
I don't follow you.

□ 뭐라고?
What?
(I'm) Sorry?
Excuse me?
I beg your pardon?

	Come again?
□ 다시 한번 반복해 줄래?	Can you repeat that?
	Can you explain that again?
□ 알기 쉽게 설명해 줄래?	Can you go over that again?
	Can you simplify that?
□ 헷갈려.	It's confusing.
	It makes me confused.
	I'm confused.
□ 굳이 말 안 해도 돼.	You don't have to say.
	You don't have to explain.
□ 나 아직 말 안 끝났어.	I'm not done yet.
	I'm not finished.
	I'm still talking.
□ 할 말 더 있는데.	I have more things to say.
	I want to say something more.
□ 말 끊지 마.	Don't stop me.
	Don't interrupt me.
□ 중간에 끼어들지 마.	Don't cut in.
	Don't break in.
□ 제발 내 말을 끝내게 해 주세요.	Please let me finish.
	Can't you let me finish?

Notes

hold 잡다, 중지하다 get at 의미하다, 말하고자 하다 get it 알다, 이해하다 go over 다시 반복하다 simplify 알기 쉽게 단순화하다(= elaborate) confusing 헷갈리게 하는, 혼란스러운 interrupt 방해하다(= intrude) cut in 끼어들다, 새치기하다(= break in)

05 오해 풀기, 사과하기

대화를 나누거나 자신의 의사를 표현할 때에는 언제든지 오해의 가능성이 있습니다. 일단 오해가 생기면 거짓말을 하거나 어색하게 사태를 악화시키는 것보다 솔직 담백한 대화로 clear things up(오해를 풀다) 혹은 get things straight(확실히 짚고 넘어가다) 할 수 있도록 노력해야겠죠.

원어민 발음 듣기 ☑□　회화 훈련 □□　듣기 훈련 □□

□ (그건) 오해야.

That's a (huge) misunderstanding.
It's a total mix-up.
You misunderstood me.
You got me wrong.

□ 오해하지 마.

Don't misunderstand me.
Don't get me wrong.

□ 그런 뜻은 아니었어.

I didn't mean it.
I didn't mean to hurt your feelings.

□ 네게 한 말이 아니야.

I wasn't saying it to you.
It wasn't meant for you.

□ 말이 허투루 나갔어.

It just slipped from my mouth.
I was thinking out loud.
You were not supposed to hear it.

□ 그냥 하는 말이었어.

It doesn't mean anything.
It meant nothing.

□ 혼잣말이었어.

I was talking to myself.

□ 오해가 있는 것 같아.

I think we have a misunderstanding.

□ 오해 풀어.

Let's clear things up.
Let's clear the air.

	Let's get things straight.
□ 어떻게 해야 네 오해가 풀릴까?	What can I do to make you feel better?
	What do you want me to do to clear things up?
	What should I do to get things straight?
□ 오해를 확대시키지 마.	Don't make a big deal out of this.
	Don't make a fuss out of this. *this → nothing (아무것도 아닌 일)
□ 툭 터놓고 얘기해 보자.	Let's have a heart-to-heart talk.
□ 솔직하게 말하지 그래?	Why don't you level with me?
□ 허심탄회하게 말할게.	I'll be completely honest with you.
	I'll level with you.

📑 Notes

misunderstanding 오해   total 완전히, 정말로   mix-up 혼란, 뒤섞임, 오해   get ~ wrong ~를 잘못 이해하다, 오해하다   mean ~을 의미하다, ~할 의도가 있다   hurt one's feelings ~의 감정을 상하게 하다   slip from one's mouth 입에서 무심코 말이 흘러나가다   think out loud 무심코 말을 내뱉다   clear things up 오해를 풀다, 제대로 하다(= clear the air, get things straight)   make ~ feel better ~의 기분을 나아지게 하다   make a big deal 일을 크게 만들다, 시끄럽게 하다(= make a fuss)   heart-to-heart 마음으로부터, 솔직한   level with ~에게 솔직하게 털어놓다

06 말다툼

MP3를 들어보세요 02-U06

의도적이든 아니든 대화 중에 말다툼이 일어나는 경우가 있습니다. 지나치다 싶은 말에는 참지 말고 You crossed the line.(도가 지나치다.)이라고 경고하세요. 간단히 "입[말] 조심해."라고 말할 때는 Watch your mouth[tongue].라고 합니다.

원어민 발음 듣기 ☑□   회화 훈련 □□   듣기 훈련 □□

□ 말이 지나치다.	It's too much.
	How can you say that?
	How can you talk to me like that?
□ 너 (넘지 말아야 할) 선을 넘었어.	You crossed the line.
	You went too far.
□ 나 기분 상했어.	You hurt my feelings.
□ 네가 상관할 바 아니야.	It's none of your business.
□ 넌 그렇게 말할 자격 없어.	You have no right to say that.
□ 말조심해.	Hey, watch!
	Watch your mouth.
	Be careful.
□ (그게) 내 탓이라는 거야?	Are you saying that it's my fault?
	Are you blaming me?
	So it's my fault?
□ 뭘 암시하는 거야?	What are you implying?
□ 말 빙빙 돌리지 마.	Stop beating around the bush.
□ 주제 바꾸지 마.	Don't change the subject.
□ 억지 부리지 마.	Don't twist my words.

▫ (그렇게) 비꼬지 마.	Don't be (so) sarcastic.
▫ 단도직입적으로 말해.	What's your point?
	Get to the point.
▫ 입 다물어!	Shut up!
	Shut your mouth!
	Zip it!
▫ 그만해!	Stop it!
	Cut it out!
	Enough!
▫ 거짓말 마!	Don't lie to me.
	Stop lying.
	You're a liar.
▫ 네 말에 가시가 있어.	Your words have a sting.
	You have a harsh tongue.
▫ 내가 왜 이런 말을 들어야 해?	Why do I have to listen to this?
	I don't need to listen to this.

Notes

cross the line 선을 넘다, 도가 지나치다(=be out of the line)   imply 암시하다, 넌지시 의미하다   beat around the bush 변죽을 울리다, 핵심을 말하지 않고 딴소리만 하다   twist one's words 억지 부리다   sarcastic 비꼬는, 야유하는, 빈정거리는   zip 채우다, 닫다   cut out 그만하다, 관두다   sting 가시, 아픈 것   harsh 거친, 혹독한

비밀에 대해 말하기

Don't tell anyone.(아무한테도 말하면 안 돼.)라고 말하면 더 빨리 퍼져나가는 비밀! 그래서 open secret(공공연한 비밀)이라는 말도 생겨났나 봅니다. 만약 비밀을 꼭 지키겠다고 다짐했다면 상대방에게 I won't tell anyone. 또는 I'll keep your secret.(비밀 지킬게.)라고 말하세요.

□ 비밀이야.	It's a secret.
□ 완전 비밀이야.	It's top-secret.
□ 극비야.	It's (strictly) confidential.
	It's (strictly) classified.
□ 공공연한 비밀이야.	It's an open secret.
	Everyone knows the secret.
□ 말 못해.	I can't tell you.
	I'm not supposed to tell you.
	I'm not allowed to say anything.
	I'm not at liberty to say this.
□ 제발 말해 줘.	Please tell me.
	Please share it with me.
□ 아무한테도 말하면 안 돼.	Don't tell anyone.
	Don't share this with anyone.
	You can't tell anyone.
	Keep it to yourself.
	Take it to your grave.
□ 아무한테도 말 안 할게.	I won't tell anyone.

□ 비밀 지킬게.	I'll keep your secret.
	My lips are sealed.
	You can trust me.
□ 나 비밀 잘 지키잖아.	I can keep secrets.
□ 비밀을 이야기할 사람도 없어.	I don't have anyone to tell.
	I have nobody to tell.
□ 우리끼리 하는 말인데.	It's just between you and me.
	It's between us.
	It's our secret.
□ 조용히 해. 누가 들을라.	Hush! Someone will hear you.
	Lower your voice.
	Keep it down.
□ 모두가 그것을 쉬쉬해.	Everyone hushes it.
□ 비밀에 부치자.	Let's keep it a secret.
	*secret = private
	Let's keep it under our hat.

Notes

strictly 엄히, 철저히   confidential 극비의, 기밀의(= classified)   be supposed to ~하기로 되어 있다   be allowed to ~하도록 허용되다   be at liberty to ~ 마음대로 ~하다   share A with B A를 B와 나누다, 공유하다   take ~ to one's grave ~을 무덤까지 가져가다, ~을 아무에게도 말하지 않다   keep ~ to oneself ~을 스스로만 알다, 간직하다   seal 눈을 꼭 감다, 입(술)을 꼭 다물다, 비밀을 간직하다   leak out 바깥으로 새다, 누출되다   keep ~ under one's hat ~을 비밀로 하다

08 뉴스(소식) 전하기

MP3를 들어보세요 02-U08

새로운 소식이나 빅뉴스로 시작하는 대화는 언제나 흥미진진합니다. 소식을 전하기 전에 You wouldn't believe this.(들어도 믿기지 않을걸)와 같은 표현으로 상대방의 호기심을 더욱 유발할 수도 있죠. 출처를 밝히고 싶지 않을 때에는 Someone told me ~(누가 그러던데 ~)로 이야기를 꺼내면 됩니다.

원어민 발음 듣기 ☑□　회화 훈련 □□　듣기 훈련 □□

깜짝 놀랄 만한 소식이 있어.	Surprise news (for you)! I have surprise news for you.
따끈따끈한 소식이야.	It's hot news.
좋은 소식과 나쁜 소식이 있어.	I have good news and bad news.
어느 것부터 들을래?	Which one do you want to hear first?
들어도 믿기지 않을걸.	You wouldn't believe (this). You wouldn't believe your ears.
새로운 소식 있어?	Any news? Anything new?
그 소식(이야기) 들었어?	Did you hear that? Did you happen to hear that?
누가 그러는데 ~	Someone told me…
소문에 ~	Rumor says… There is a rumor (that)…
확실한 이야기야.	I heard from the horse's mouth.
나쁜 소식이 더 빨리 퍼져.	Bad news travels quickly.

09 농담하기

적절한 유머는 대화가 잘 이어져 나갈 수 있도록 만드는 윤활유 역할을 합니다. 물론 그 정도가 심해 상대방이 자신을 놀리고 있다는 느낌이 들 정도로 불쾌감을 주어서는 안 되겠죠. 농담을 그만하라고 경고할 때는 Stop kidding around.(농담 그만해.) 또는 I'm not up for a joke.(농담할 기분 아니야.)라고 말합니다.

원어민 발음 듣기 ✔️☐   회화 훈련 ☐☐   듣기 훈련 ☐☐

□ 농담이야.
I'm kidding.
*kidding = joking
It is a joke.

□ 농담이지?
You're kidding, right?
You're pulling my leg, right?
It was a joke, right?

□ 농담 그만해.
Stop kidding around.

□ 그만 좀 놀려 대.
Stop teasing me.
Stop playing with me.
Don't make fun of me.

□ 농담 아니야.
I'm not kidding.
It's not a joke.
I'm serious.

□ 농담이야 진담이야?
Are you kidding or what?
Are you serious or what?

□ 농담 반 진담 반이야.
Half in joke.
Half for fun.

□ 농담할 기분 아니야.
I'm not in the mood for a joke.
I don't feel like joking around.
I'm not up for a joke.

□ 농담으로 알아들을게.	I'll take it as a joke.
□ 그만 좀 웃겨.	Oh, stop!
	Stop making me laugh.
	Stop cracking me up.
□ 뭐가 그렇게 재미있어?	What's so funny?

  Notes

pull one's leg 놀리다   tease 놀리다, 괴롭히다   make fun of 놀리다, 괴롭히다   or what? 아니면 뭐야?   be in the mood for ~할 기분이다   feel like ~할 것 같다   be up for ~을 하려고 하다   take A as B A를 B로 받아들이다   crack up 박장대소하게 하다

뒷담화

뒤에서 남의 흉을 보는 talking behind someone's back(뒷담화하기)은 죄책감을 느끼면서도 은근히 즐기게 되는 대화입니다. 하지만 Walls have ears.(벽에도 귀가 있다.)라는 사실을 절대 잊어서는 안 됩니다.

원어민 발음 듣기 ☑☐　회화 훈련 ☐☐　듣기 훈련 ☐☐

□ 뒷담화하지 마.　　Don't talk behind someone's back.
　　　　　　　　　Don't speak ill of others behind their back.
　　　　　　　　　Don't backbite someone.

□ 뒤에서 그를 흉보다가 들켰어.　I got caught while backbiting him.

□ 그는 뒷담화가 심해.　He is a serious backbiter.
　　　　　　　　　　He always backbites others.

□ 그들은 남 말 하기를 좋아해.　They are very gossipy.
　　　　　　　　　　　　　They love (all kinds of) gossip.

□ 벽에도 귀가 있어.　Walls have ears.

□ 그녀는 평판이 나빠.　She has a bad reputation.
　　　　　　　　　　She has an ill name.

□ 그는 왕따야.　He is being bullied.
　　　　　　　He is picked on by others.
　　　　　　　He is a loser.

□ 할 말 있으면 내 앞에서 해.　If you have something to say, say it in front of me.

Chapter 03

의견
Opinion

01 의견 제시하기 02 확신과 결심에 대한 표현 03 질문과 대답
04 찬성과 반대 05 설득하기 06 제안의 수락과 거절

01 의견 제시하기

MP3를 들어보세요 03-U01

자신의 의견을 제대로 표현하는 것은 대화에서 매우 중요합니다. 의견을 제시할 때는 I think… 또는 In my opinion… 등으로 말을 시작합니다. 의견을 제시하면서 정중하게 양해를 구할 때는 Can I say a word?(제가 한마디 해도 될까요?)라고 하면 되죠.

원어민 발음 듣기 ☑□　회화 훈련 □□　듣기 훈련 □□

□ 제 생각에는 ~	I think…
	In my opinion…
	My opinion is…

| □ 제가 보기에는 ~ | As I see it… |
| | The way I see it… |

| □ 제 관점에서는 ~ | In my view… |
| | My point of view is… |

| □ 좋은 아이디어가 있는데요. | I have an idea. |
| | Here's an idea. |

| □ 문득 떠오른 생각인데요. | An idea just came to my mind. |
| | An idea just crossed my mind. |

□ 한마디(몇 마디) 해도 될까요?	Can I say a word?
	Can I say a few words?
	I would like to say a word.
	Mind if I say something?

| □ 제안을 하나 해도 될까요? | Can I make a suggestion? |

📋 Notes

point of view 관점　come to one's mind 생각이 문득 떠오르다　cross one's mind 생각이 문득 스쳐 지나다　Mind if ~? ~해도 될까요?　make a suggestion 제안(제의)하다

확신과 결심에 대한 표현

확신을 나타내는 표현으로 I'm sure that ~ (~은 확실해요)이 가장 흔하게 쓰입니다. 한편 "결심했어요.", "아직 결심이 서지 않았어요." 등은 과거에서부터 고민하여 현재 결심한 상태 또는 결심하지 못한 상태에 이르렀음을 표현해야 하므로 꼭 have[has]+과거분사[현재완료]와 함께 씁니다.

원어민 발음 듣기 ☑☐ 회화 훈련 ☐☐ 듣기 훈련 ☐☐

□ ~은 확실해요.

I'm (pretty) sure that…
There is no doubt that…

□ ~은 확실치 않아요.

I'm not sure that…
I can't guarantee you that…

□ 확실해? / 자신해?

Are you sure?
*sure = certain, positive, confident
Are you 100% sure about this?
(You) Swear?

□ 당연해요. / 물론이죠.

Absolutely!
Certainly!
Definitely!
Sure!
Positive!

□ 맹세해요.

I swear to god.
Cross my heart.

□ 두말할 필요도 없이 ~

Needless to say…

□ 저만 믿으세요.

Trust me.
You can count on me.
*count on = rely on
You have my word.

□ 저에게 맡기세요.	I'll take care of it.
	I'll handle it.
	Leave it to me.
□ 결심했어요.	I've made up my mind.
	I've finally come to the decision.
	My mind is all set.
□ 결심(결정)하기 힘들어요.	It's very hard to decide.
	It's very difficult to make up my mind.
□ 아직 결심이 서지 않았어요.	I haven't decided yet.
	I haven't made up my mind yet.
□ 어떻게 해야 할지 모르겠어요.	I don't know what to do.
	I'm totally lost.
□ 마음이 바뀌었어요.	I've changed my mind.
	I'm having a second thought.
□ 한번 해 봅시다.	Let's do it.
	Let's give it a shot.
	Let's go for it.
	Why don't we try?
□ 후회하지 않아요.	I won't regret this.
	I won't look back.

📋 Notes

guarantee 장담하다, 보장하다 swear 맹세하다, 확신하다 cross one's heart 맹세하다, 확신하다 have one's word 약속하다, 믿어도 되다 take care of 돌보다, 해결하다 make up one's mind 결심하다, 결정하다 come to the decision 결심하다, 결정하다 second thought 재고, 다시 생각함 give it a shot 한번 해 보다, 부딪쳐 보다 go for it 사생결단으로 한번 해 보다 look back 돌아보다, 후회하다

03 질문과 대답

의견을 주고받는 과정에서 질문과 대답은 필수적입니다. 하지만 질문에 답하고 싶지 않을 경우 I don't want to answer it.(대답하고 싶지 않아요.)이라고 분명하게 말하세요. 말문이 막힐 때는 Hmm. 또는 Let's see.라고 하며 생각할 시간을 버는 것도 좋은 방법입니다.

원어민 발음 듣기 ☑□ 회화 훈련 □□ 듣기 훈련 □□

□ 이것에 대해 어떻게 생각해요? What do you think about this?
What is your opinion on this?
I would like to have your opinion.
Let's talk about this.
Any ideas?

□ 다른 의견 있어요? Does anyone have other opinions?
Does anyone have other suggestions?
Any other ideas?
Any other suggestions?
Any other comments?

□ 추가하고 싶은 사람 있어요? Does anyone want to add more?
Anybody want to add something?

□ 질문이 있으면 손드세요. If you have any questions, raise your hand.

□ 부끄러워하지 마세요. Don't be shy.

□ 마음껏 질문하세요. Feel free to ask any questions.
Ask anything.

□ 주저 말고 질문하세요. Don't hesitate to ask.

☐ 네, 질문 있어요.	Yes, I have a question.
	Yes, I want to ask something.
☐ 그 점에 대해 설명할게요.	I'll explain it.
	I have an explanation for that.
☐ 자세히 설명할게요.	I will explain more in detail.
	I will tell you more details.
☐ 예를 들어 설명할게요.	I will explain with examples.
☐ 좋은 질문이에요.	Good question!
☐ 반가운 질문이네요.	Glad you ask.
☐ 대답하고 싶지 않아요.	I don't want to answer it.
	I'm not going to answer it.
	No need to answer it.
☐ 할 말 없어요.	I have nothing to say.
	No comment on that.
☐ 뭐라 말해야 할지 모르겠어요.	I don't know what to say.
	I'm speechless.
☐ 잠시만요.	Give me a moment.
	One second, please.
☐ 그게, 그러니까…….	Let's see…
	Hmm.
	Well.
	What I'm trying to say is…

📄 Notes

suggestion 제안, 제시   comment 말, 의견   raise one's hand 손들다   feel free to 마음껏 ~하다   hesitate 주저하다, 망설이다   in detail 자세히, 상세히

찬성과 반대

상대방의 의견에 전적으로 찬성 또는 반대할 때 totally, completely 등과 같은 부사를 쓸 수 있습니다. '적극 찬성'의 의미로 100%도 자주 쓰입니다. 반대할 때는 '미안하지만', '안타깝게도', '일리는 있지만', '이렇게 말하기는 싫지만' 등의 부드러운 표현과 함께 쓰는 것이 좋습니다.

원어민 발음 듣기 ☑□　회화 훈련 □□　듣기 훈련 □□

□ 당신 말이 맞아요.
You're (absolutely) right.
*right = correct

□ 일리가 있어요.
You have a point.
You've got a point.

□ 찬성해요.
I agree with you.
I'm with you.

□ 전적으로 찬성해요.
I agree with you 100%.
I'm with you 100%.
I couldn't agree with you more.
I totally agree with you.
*totally = completely, absolutely, entirely

□ 찬성하는 부분이 있어요.
I agree with you partly.
I don't disagree entirely.

□ 그건 말도 안 돼요.
You're wrong.
You're completely wrong about this.
That's ridiculous.

□ 반대해요.
I disagree.
I don't agree with you.

☐ 미안하지만 찬성할 수 없어요.	I'm sorry but I can't agree with you.
	I'm afraid I can't agree with you.
	I hate to say this but I disagree.
☐ 일리가 있지만 찬성할 수 없어요.	You have a point but I disagree.
☐ 당신 말이 맞는다고 쳐요.	Let's say you're right.
☐ 미심쩍어요.	I doubt it.
	I have my doubt.
☐ 적극 반대해요.	I totally disagree.
	I couldn't disagree with you more.
	I'm strongly against it.
☐ 전 중립이에요.	I'm in the middle (position).
☐ 논란의 여지가 있어요.	It's debatable.
	*debatable = disputable
☐ 무작정 반대하지만 마세요.	Don't just say no.
☐ 반대를 위한 반대는 하지 마세요.	Don't say no for no.
☐ 그런 결론은 위험한데요.	That conclusion can be risky.
☐ 여론에 휩쓸리지 마세요.	Don't yield to the majority.
	Don't be overwhelmed by other people.

📑 Notes

absolutely 완전히, 전적으로　have a point 말에 일리가 있다, 동의하는 바가 있다 (= have got a point)　partly 부분적으로(= partially)　ridiculous 말도 안 되는, 터무니없는　debatable 논란의 여지가 있는(= disputable)　risky 위험스러운, 모험의 여지가 있는　yield 양보하다, 굴복하다　majority 과반수, 다수, 여론　be overwhelmed 압도당하다, 완전 주눅 들다　have a meeting 미팅을 갖다, 미팅하다

05 설득하기

대화 중에 상대방과 의견 차가 생기면 상대를 설득하기 위해 Think again. 혹은 Please reconsider.라고 말합니다. 손익을 다시 한번 따져 보며 room for comprise(타협의 여지)를 찾기 위해서입니다. 이렇게 해서 서로에게 최상의 결론을 찾는다면 더할 나위 없이 좋겠죠.

원어민 발음 듣기 ☑☐   회화 훈련 ☐☐   듣기 훈련 ☐☐

□ 재고해 주세요.	Think again.
	Think it over.
	Please reconsider.
	Why don't you think again?
□ 신중히 생각해 보세요.	Give it a serious thought.
	Think twice.
□ 다시 생각해 볼게요.	I'll think again.
	I'll give it a second thought.
□ 마음속을 잘 들여다보세요.	Look inside of your heart.
□ 제가 이야기하고 싶은 것은 ~	All I'm saying is that…
	My point is that…
□ 이익을 잘 따져 보세요.	Think carefully what you're going to get.
□ 저라면 (단연) 그렇게 할 겁니다.	If I were you, I (definitely) would do that.
□ 먼 미래를 보세요.	Think about the future.
	Don't be short-sighted.

제안의 수락과 거절

이번에는 상대방의 제안을 accept(수락하다)하고 refuse(거절하다)하는 표현을 알아봅시다. 수락할 때는 기쁜 마음으로 I'd love to. 혹은 Sounds lovely.라고 하고, 거절할 때는 정중하고 명확하게 I'm sorry but I have to say no.라고 말해야 오해가 없습니다.

~하실래요?	Would you like to…?
	Do you want to…?
~할지 궁금하네요.	I'm wondering if you could…
	I wonder if you can…
	*if = whether
~할까 생각 중인데요.	I'm thinking that…
같이 갈래요?	Would you like to come?
	Want to come?
저희와 함께 하실래요?	Want to join us?
좋아요, 그러죠.	Of course.
	Definitely.
	Certainly.
	Sure, why not?
	I'd love to.
	Sounds lovely.
	*lovely = great
	I'm in.
글쎄요, 생각해 볼게요.	Well, I'll think about it.
	Well, I have to think about it.
먼저 일정을 볼게요.	Let me check my schedule first.

☐ 지금 당장 답해야 해요?	Do I have to answer right now?
	Do you need my answer right now?
☐ 시간을 좀 주세요.	Give us some time.
☐ 사람들과 의논해 볼게요.	I need to talk to my people.
☐ 조만간 알려줄게요.	I'll let you know soon.
☐ 전화할게요.	I'll call you.
	*call→contact(연락하다)
☐ 해 보도록 할게요.	I'll try.
	I'll do my best.
☐ 미안하지만 거절할게요.	I'm sorry, but I have to say no.
	I have to pass.
	Sorry, but not this time.
☐ 너무 좋지만 안 되겠어요.	I'd love to but I can't.
	It's a tempting offer, but I can't accept it.
	Sounds great, but I can't.
	I wish I could.
☐ 다음에요.	Maybe next time.
	Maybe some other time.
	Maybe later.
	Rain check?
	Next time, I'm definitely in.

Notes

Would you like to ~? ~을 원하세요?, ~하고 싶으세요?(= Do you want to ~?) wonder if ~인지 아닌지 궁금하다(=whether) give ~ time ~에게 시간(여유, 말미)을 주다 one's people ~의 사람들, ~의 측근들 do one's best 최선을 다하다 tempting 끌리는, 매혹적인 rain check 후일의 약속, 다음 기회

Chapter 04

감정 표현
Emotion

01 기쁨, 즐거움, 감동 02 슬픔 03 우울함, 외로움 04 낙담, 후회
05 위로, 격려 06 불쾌함, 화남 07 (상대방에 대한) 비난 08 (자신에 대한) 불평, 불만
09 싸움 10 긴장, 초조 11 두려움, 놀람 12 창피, 당황스러움
13 귀찮음, 성가심 14 그리움 15 걱정, 근심 16 의심

기쁨, 즐거움, 감동

사람의 감정을 나타내는 표현들 중 기쁨, 즐거움 등을 나타내는 표현을 배워 보겠습니다. 가장 일반적인 표현인 I'm so happy.(너무 기뻐.)에서부터 큰 감동을 표현하는 I'm so happy and that I could cry.(너무 기뻐서 울 것 같아.)까지 다양한 표현들을 익혀 보세요.

원어민 발음 듣기 ☑☐   회화 훈련 ☐☐   듣기 훈련 ☐☐

□ (매우) 기쁘다.
I'm (so) happy.
I feel happy.
*happy = delighted, glad, pleased
I'm in paradise.

□ 그건 나를 기쁘게 해.
It makes me happy.

□ 신나. / 즐거워.
I'm excited.
I'm thrilled.
I feel awesome.

□ 기분 끝내줘.
Couldn't be happier.

□ 만족스러워.
I'm satisfied.
I'm content.

□ 대만족이야.
I'm very satisfied.
*satisfied = contented

□ 기쁨으로 가슴이 벅차.
My heart is full of happiness.
My heart is overflowing with joy.

□ 꿈만 같아.
Is this a dream?
I feel like dreaming.
It's like a dream come true.
I hope it's not a dream.
Don't wake up.

▫ 마음이 (마구) 설레.	My heart is beating (so fast).
	My heart is throbbing.
▫ 너무 기뻐서 울 것 같아.	I'm so happy that I could cry.
▫ 너무 기뻐서 말이 안 나와.	I'm so happy that I can't talk.
▫ 구름 위에 있는 것 같아.	I'm on cloud nine.
	I'm floating on air.
	*floating = walking, treading
▫ 입이 귀에 걸렸네.	You're smiling from ear to ear.
▫ 요즘 싱글벙글하네.	You're all smiles these days.
▫ 기쁨을 감출 수가 없어.	I can't hide my happiness.
▫ 자꾸 웃음이 나와.	I keep smiling.
	I can't help smiling.
▫ 너무 웃어서 배가 아파.	My stomach hurts.
	My sides hurt.
▫ 기분 좋아 보인다.	You look happy.
▫ 뭐 기분 좋은 일 있어?	What are you so happy about?
	Any good news?
	Something good happened to you.
▫ 뭐가 그렇게 재미있어?	What's so funny?
▫ 좋은 소식은 함께 나누자.	Let's share the good news.
▫ 웃음은 전염돼.	Laughter is contagious.

📖 Notes

thrilled 신나는, 몹시 흥분되는 awesome 멋진, 최고의 overflow 넘치다, 벅차다 come true 실현되다 beat 때리다, 고동치다 throb 욱신거리다, 설레다 cloud nine (구름 위에 있는 듯) 기분이 매우 좋은 tread 밟다, 걷다 contagious 전염성이 있는, 옮는

02 슬픔

'슬프고 눈물이 날 것 같은' 기분을 표현할 때 항상 sad만 써 왔나요? 슬픔이 아주 클 때 "가슴이 아프다.", "가슴이 찢어진다."라고 말하기도 하는데, 이것은 My heart hurts. 또는 My heart is broken.이라고 합니다. 이번에는 슬픔의 감정을 나타내는 다양한 표현들을 알아봅시다.

원어민 발음 듣기 ☑□　　회화 훈련 □□　　듣기 훈련 □□

☐ (너무) 슬퍼.	I'm (so) sad. I feel (so) sad. *sad = miserable
☐ 넌 나를 슬프게 해.	You make me miserable.
☐ 너 슬퍼 보여.	You look sad. Are you sad? Why do you look sad? Something's wrong?
☐ 가슴(마음)이 아파.	My heart hurts. It hurts my heart.
☐ 가슴(마음)이 찢어져.	My heart is broken. I feel heartbroken.
☐ 가슴에 사무쳐.	It touches my heart. It went to my heart.
☐ 가슴이 뭉클했어.	I felt a lump in my throat.
☐ (슬픔으로) 목이 메었어.	I was choked up.
☐ (엉엉) 울고만 싶어.	I just want to cry (out loud). I feel like crying (out loud).
☐ 왜 울고 있니?	Why are you crying?

□ 눈물이 쏟아졌어.	Tears poured down my cheeks.
□ 와락 울음이 터졌어.	I burst into tears. *burst into = break into
□ 눈이 퉁퉁 붓도록 울었어.	I cried my eyes out.
□ 아직도 눈물이 나.	I'm still in tears. It still brings tears to my eyes. My eyes all tear up.
□ 너무 슬퍼하지 마.	Don't be so sad. Don't feel so sad.
□ 실컷 울어.	Cry yourself out. Cry your heart out. Let it all out.
□ 밤새 울었어.	I cried all night.
□ 울다 지쳐 잠들었어.	I cried myself to sleep. I fell asleep while crying.

Notes

miserable 슬픈, 불행한, 비참한   heartbroken 슬픔에 잠긴, 비탄에 젖은   touch 감동을 주다, 사무치게 하다   lump 덩어리   throat 목, 목구멍   be choked up 목이 메다   pour down 쏟아져 내리다   burst into 와락 터지다, 터져 나오다   tear up 눈물이 글썽글썽하다   cry out 실컷 울다, 엉엉 울다   let out 내놓다, 드러내다

03 우울함, 외로움

depressed, blue, down 등은 '울적한' 기분을 나타내는 형용사들입니다. 특히 the blues 하면 '울적한 기분', '무거운 기분'을 뜻하죠. 월요일에 특히 몸과 마음이 축 처지는 '월요병'을 Monday blues라고 부르는 것도 그 때문입니다.

원어민 발음 듣기 ☑□   회화 훈련 □□   듣기 훈련 □□

□ (많이) 우울해.
I'm (very) depressed.
I feel (very) depressed.
I'm heavy-hearted.
I'm (so) blue.
I have the blues.
I feel down.

□ 우울해 보여.
You look depressed.
*depressed = melancholy, down, blue, heavy-hearted

□ 날씨 탓인가.
Maybe it's (because of) the weather.

□ 컨디션이 별로야.
I don't feel good.
I'm under the weather.

□ 아무것도 재미없어.
Nothing interests me.
I lost interest in life.

□ 늘 기운이 없어.
I always feel tired.
I'm groggy all the time.

□ 노력하면 뭐 해.
Why all the trying?
*trying = troubles, efforts
What for?
Why bother?

☐ 시원섭섭해.	I feel relieved, but sad at the same time.
☐ 달콤 쌉싸름해.	It's bittersweet.
☐ (너무) 허전해.	I feel (so) empty. *empty = hollow, vain My life is (so) empty.
☐ (너무) 외로워. / 쓸쓸해.	I'm (very) lonely. I feel (so) lonely.
☐ 혼자 있기 싫어.	I don't want to be alone. I don't want to be left alone.
☐ 소외된 느낌이야.	I feel (so) isolated. *isolated = alienated
☐ 방치된 느낌이야.	I feel (so) neglected.
☐ 누군가와 이야기 나누고 싶어.	I want to talk to someone. I need someone to talk to.
☐ 월요병이야.	It's Monday blues.
☐ 사춘기야.	It's teenage blues.
☐ 명절 증후군이야.	It's holiday blues. *holiday → party (파티)

Notes

depressed 우울한, 울적한 heavy-hearted 마음이 무거운, 울적한 groggy 피곤한, 기운 없어 휘청거리는 relieved 안도하는, 한숨 돌리는 left alone 혼자 남겨진 isolated 고립된, 소외된(=alienated) neglected 방치된, 혼자 남겨진 speaking of ~ ~ 이야기가 나와서 말인데 cheer oneself up 스스로 기운을 북돋우다, 힘내다, 용기 내다

04 낙담, 후회

원하는 바가 잘 되지 않아 낙담하거나 실망하여 급기야 후회를 거듭하는 일이 종종 있습니다. "실망이야.", "절망적이야.", "후회스러워."와 같은 말을 어떻게 표현하는지, 그리고 후회(~했어야 했는데, ~하지 말았어야 했는데)를 나타내는 should (not) have+과거분사는 어떻게 활용하는지 살펴보겠습니다.

원어민 발음 듣기 ☑☐   회화 훈련 ☐☐   듣기 훈련 ☐☐

□ (매우) 실망이야.
I'm (very) disappointed.
It's (very) discouraging.

□ 실망스럽겠다!
You must be disappointed.
*disappointed = discouraged
It must be disappointing.
I think I understand your disappointment.

□ 너는 나를 실망시켰어.
You disappointed me.
You let me down.
You crushed my hope.
You burst a bubble.

□ 절망적이야.
It's hopeless.
It's disastrous.
I'm desperate.
I'm giving up all hope.

□ 죽고만 싶어.
I just want to die.

□ 나 자신에게 실망스러워.
I disappointed myself.
I let myself down.

□ 실망하지 마.
Don't be so disappointed.

□ 실망시키지 마.	Don't you ever disappoint me. *disappoint = discourage Never ever let me down.
□ 후회스러워.	I feel regret. I feel remorse. I'm regretful. *regretful = remorseful
□ 모든 게 끝이야.	It's all over. It's done. It's the end.
□ 네가 할 수 있는 일은 없어.	There's nothing you can do.
□ 난 끝났어.	I'm finished. I'm through. I'm screwed. I'm dead.
□ 그쯤은 예상했어야 했는데…….	I should have known better.
□ 난 낙오자야.	I'm a loser. I'm a total failure.
□ 다시 기회가 올까?	Will I have a second chance? I wonder if there's another chance. I hope there's another chance.

📑 Notes

let ~ down ~를 실망시키다 burst a bubble 거품을 터뜨리다, 희망을 깨다 disastrous 절망적인 remorse 후회, 양심의 가책 be over 끝나다, 끝장나다, 종결되다 screwed 엉망이 된, 망친 loser 패배자, 낙오자

05 위로, 격려

슬픈 일을 겪고 있는 사람에게 진심이 담긴 위로와 격려는 큰 힘이 될 수 있습니다. I'm so sorry.(정말 안됐네요.), It's nothing.(아무것도 아닌 일이에요.), Don't blame yourself.(자책하지 마세요.) 등의 표현을 사용해 보세요.

원어민 발음 듣기 ☑☐   회화 훈련 ☐☐   듣기 훈련 ☐☐

□ 정말 안됐네요.
I'm so sorry (to hear that).
I feel so sorry for…
I feel pity for…
*for 뒤에는 무엇 때문에 안됐는지가 나온다.

□ 어떻게 견디고 계세요?
How are you holding up?
It must be tough for you.

□ 포기하지 마세요.
Don't give up.
Keep trying.

□ 다 잘될 거예요.
Everything will be fine.
*fine = okay, all right

□ 과거는 과거예요.
(What's) Done is done.
The past is in the past.

□ 다 잊어버리세요.
Forget about everything.

□ 아무것도 아닌 일이에요.
It's nothing.
It's not a big deal.
It's no biggy.

□ 자신을 과소평가하지 마세요.
Don't underestimate yourself.
You are (much) more than that.

□ 자책하지 말아요.
Don't blame yourself.
Don't be so harsh on you.

☐ 당신 탓이 아니에요.	It's not (entirely) your fault.
☐ 천천히 생각하세요.	Take things slowly.
☐ 한숨 자면 기분이 나아질 거예요.	Take a nap and you will feel better.
☐ 내 어깨를 빌려 줄게요.	I'll give you my shoulder. You have my shoulder.
☐ 기운 내세요.	Cheer up! Pep up! Chin up! Pull yourself together.
☐ 세상이 끝난 것이 아니에요.	It's not the end of the world.
☐ 시간이 약이에요.	Time will cure you.
☐ 좋은 날이 올 거예요.	Good days will come.
☐ 쥐구멍에도 볕들 날이 있어요.	Every dog has his day.
☐ 내일은 또 다른 날이잖아요.	Tomorrow is another day.
☐ 다른 기회가 올 거예요.	You'll have a second chance.
☐ 긍정적인 면을 보세요.	Look on the bright side. Try to be positive. Think positively.
☐ 당신을 위해 기원할게요.	I'll pray for you. I'll cross my fingers.
☐ 나중 일은 나중에 걱정해요.	Worry next time next time.

📑 Notes

hold up 견디다, 지탱하다   underestimate oneself 스스로를 과소평가하다   blame oneself 자책하다   be harsh on ~ ~에게 혹독하게 대하다   chin up 기운 내다   pull oneself together 기운을 찾다, 냉정해지다   cross one's fingers 기원하다

06 불쾌함, 화남

기분이 나쁘고 화나는 감정은 기쁨이나 즐거움만큼 격한 감정들이죠. 단순히 I feel bad.(기분 나빠.), I feel unpleasant.(불쾌해.), I'm so angry.(열 받아.)뿐 아니라 Steam is coming out of my ear.(머리에서 김 나네.), It drives me crazy.(돌아 버리겠네.)와 같이 다양한 표현 방법이 있습니다.

원어민 발음 듣기 ☑☐   회화 훈련 ☐☐   듣기 훈련 ☐☐

□ 기분 나빠.	I feel bad.
	It's offensive.
□ 불쾌해.	I feel unpleasant.
	I feel uncomfortable.
□ 역겨워.	It's disgusting.
	I feel disgusted.
	You disgust me.
□ (아주) 열 받아. / 화나.	I'm (so) angry.
	I'm mad.
	I'm pissed.
	I'm fuming.
	It makes me sick.
□ 열 받게 하지 마.	Don't make me angry.
	*angry = mad, furious, pissed
□ 생각할수록 열 받네.	The more I think, the more I get angry.
□ 돌아 버리겠어.	It makes me crazy.
	It drives me nuts.
	*nuts = mad, insane
□ 스트레스 받아.	I'm stressed out.

□ 가슴이 답답해.	I feel choked up.
	I feel frustrated.
	I could explode.
□ 바람 좀 쐬어야겠어.	I need fresh air.
	I'll go and get some fresh air.
□ 내가 기분 나쁘게 했어?	Did I do something to make you feel uncomfortable?
□ 농담할 기분이 아냐.	I'm not in the mood for joking.
□ 왜 나한테 화풀이야?	Why are you taking your anger out on me?
	Don't take your anger out on me.
□ 걔 (화나서) 펄펄 뛰고 있어.	He is jumping up and down.
□ 걔 (화나서) 얼굴이 시뻘개졌어.	He turns (all) red.
□ 그는 노발대발하고 있어.	He is in hot anger.
□ 그녀는 걸핏하면 화를 내.	She easily gets angry.
	She is quick-tempered.
	She is hotheaded.
□ 화를 참을 수가 없어.	I can't control my anger.
	I have an anger management problem.
□ 더 이상은 못 참아.	That's it.
	I've had enough.
	I can't take it anymore.

📝 Notes

fume 연기를 내다, 노발대발하다 nuts 미친(= insane) choked up 목이 메이는, 답답한 frustrated 좌절감을 느끼는 take ~ out on someone ~을 누군가에게 쏟아내다, 화풀이하다 ceiling 지붕, 천장 hotheaded 성질이 급한 anger management 화를 다스리기

(상대방에 대한) 비난

상대방에 대한 가벼운 질책이 불가피한 상황이 있습니다. 그럴 때는 Snap out of it!(정신 차려!), You're so naïve.(순진하기는.), Grow up!(철 좀 들어!), I knew it.(그럴 줄 알았어.)과 같이 말할 수 있습니다.

□ 정신 차려.	Snap out of it.
	Focus!
	Concentrate!
	Collect yourself.
□ 꿈 깨.	Wake up!
	Dream on!
	Get real!
	Reality check!
□ 어리석기는!	You're foolish.
	Such a fool!
□ 무식하기는!	So ignorant!
□ 몰상식해.	You have no common sense.
□ 나잇값 좀 해.	Act your age.
□ 네가 몇 살인지 알아?	How old are you?
□ 주제를 알아야지.	(You should) Know your place.
□ 철 좀 들어.	Grow up!
□ 내가 뭐랬어.	I told you (so).
□ 내가 경고했지.	I warned you.
	I was trying to warn you.

그럴 줄 알았어.	I knew it.
내 말은 절대 안 들으니까.	You never listen to me.
네 탓이야.	It's all your fault.
(잘못을) 인정해.	Admit it.
네가 책임져.	It's your responsibility. You're responsible for it.
순진하기는!	You're naive!
무신경하기는!	So insensible!
평소에 생각이 없어.	You don't think. Use your head.
넌 항상 투덜거려.	You always complain.
똑같은 말을 반복하고 있잖아.	You're saying the same thing over and over. You're like a broken record. You're singing the same song.
몇 번이나 말해야 알아들어?	How many times do I have to tell you?
건방져.	You, smart ass. You're acting fresh.
뻔뻔해.	Some nerve! You're shameless.
우는소리 하지 마.	Don't be such a crybaby.

Notes

snap out of ~에서 벗어나다, 제정신을 차리다   naive 순진한, 세상물정 모르는   broken record (고장 난 레코드처럼) 같은 이야기를 반복하는 사람   fresh 주제 넘는, 건방진   nerve 뻔뻔스러움, 철면피

(자신에 대한) 불평, 불만

스스로에게, 혹은 자신의 삶에 대해 투덜투덜 불평, 불만을 늘어놓는 경우가 있습니다. 간혹 일이 너무 풀리지 않을 때 Life is unfair.(삶은 불공평해.), Why me?(왜 하필 나야!)와 같은 말을 하고 싶을 때도 있고요. 불평, 불만에 대한 다양한 표현들을 알아보겠습니다.

원어민 발음 듣기 ☑☐　회화 훈련 ☐☐　듣기 훈련 ☐☐

☐ 삶은 불공평해.　　　　　　Life is unfair.

☐ 왜 하필 나야!　　　　　　　Why me?

☐ 시간 낭비만 했어.　　　　　It's a waste of my time.
　　　　　　　　　　　　　　What a waste of my time!

☐ 일진 사나운 날이야.　　　　I had a bad day.
　　　　　　　　　　　　　　What a bad day!

☐ 사람들이 날 대하는 방식이 싫어.　I don't like the way people treat me.

☐ 너무 피곤해.　　　　　　　I'm so tired.
　　　　　　　　　　　　　　I'm so exhausted.

☐ 넌더리가 나.　　　　　　　I'm sick and tired (of it).
　　　　　　　　　　　　　　I'm fed up (with it).

☐ 나 바보 아닌데.　　　　　　I'm not a fool.
　　　　　　　　　　　　　　I'm not stupid.

☐ (내 욕을 하는지) 귀가 간지러워.　My ears are burning.

 Notes

treat 대하다, 대접하다　exhausted 지친, 탈진한　be fed up with ~에 넌더리가 나다

09 싸움

시비가 붙어 급기야 싸움으로 번질 때 You're dead.(너 죽었어.)나 You want a piece of me?(한 판 붙자.) 같은 말을 하죠. 다음 표현들은 직접 쓰기보다 누군가가 나에게 시비를 걸 때 대응용으로 알아두면 좋습니다.

원어민 발음 듣기 ☑□   회화 훈련 □□   듣기 훈련 □□

□ 뭘 쳐다보는 거야?	What are you looking at?
□ 왜 시비야?	What's the matter with you?
	What's your problem?
	Are you picking a fight with me?
□ 일부러 그랬지?	You did it on purpose, right?
□ 먼저 사과해.	Apologize to me, first.
	You owe me an apology.
□ 멍청한 놈!	You, idiot!
□ 네까짓 게 뭐라고.	Who do you think you are?
□ 한판 붙자!	Let's do this.
	You want a piece of me?
	You want to take me?
□ 너 죽었어.	You're dead.
□ 소리 지르지 마.	Don't yell at me.
	Don't raise your voice at me.
□ 경고한다.	I'm warning you.

Notes

pick a fight 시비를 걸다   owe 빚지다   raise one's voice 목소리를 높이다, 소리 지르다

10 긴장, 초조

긴장하고 초조하면 가슴이 두근거리고(heart is pounding) 식은땀이 나면서(sweating) 가만히 있지 못하고 서성거리거나(hovering) 손톱을 물어뜯고(biting nails) 다리를 떨기도(shaking legs) 합니다. 화장실을 자주 가고 싶게 만드는 것도 긴장과 초조함의 증상이라고 하네요.

원어민 발음 듣기 ☑□　회화 훈련 □□　듣기 훈련 □□

□ 긴장돼.
I'm nervous.
It's nerve wrecking.

□ 떨려.
I'm shaking.
I have the jitters.

□ 긴장하지 마.
Don't be anxious.

□ 실수하면 어쩌지?
What if I make a mistake?

□ 너무 긴장한 것 같다.
You look very nervous.
You look too tense.

□ 마음을 느긋하게 가져.
Try to relax.
Try to be calm.

□ 잠시 다른 생각을 해 봐.
Think something else for a while.
Put it away from your mind.

□ 손톱 깨물지 마.
Stop biting your nails.

□ 그만 서성거려.
Stop hovering.
Would you quit hovering?

📑 Notes

nerve wrecking 긴장되는, 진땀 나는　the jitters 신경과민, 안전부절못함　tense 긴장된, 팽팽　put away 치워두다, 밀쳐두다　hover 정처 없이 서성거리다　blink 눈을 깜박이다

11 두려움, 놀람

두렵거나 무서운 감정은 형용사 scared, afraid, frightened 등으로 표현합니다. 너무 놀라 "충격 먹었다."라는 말은 I'm shocked. 또는 It's traumatic.이라고 하면 됩니다. 놀라서 "심장이 멎는 줄 알았어."는 I thought my heart stopped.라고 하고, "눈이 휘둥그레졌어."는 My eyes were popped.라고 합니다.

원어민 발음 듣기 ☑□   회화 훈련 □□   듣기 훈련 □□

□ (너무) 무서워.	I'm (so) scared.
	I'm afraid.
	I'm frightened.
	I'm terrified.
□ 쇼크 받았어.	I'm shocked.
	It's shocking.
□ 섬뜩해.	It's spooky.
□ 소름 끼쳐.	I've got some goose bumps.
	It gives me goose bumps.
□ 너무 무서워서 꼼짝도 못하겠어.	I'm so scared and I can't move.
□ 무서워하지 마.	Don't be scared.
	*scared = afraid, frightened
□ 큰일 날 뻔했다.	It was close.
	It was a close call.
□ 웬 날벼락이야.	That was quite unexpected.
	*unexpected = sudden
	That was out of the blue.
□ 심장이 멎는 줄 알았어.	I thought my heart stopped.

☐ 눈이 휘둥그레졌어.	My eyes were popped.
	I was pop-eyed.
☐ (너무 놀라) 뭐라고?	What?
☐ 방금 뭐라고 했어?	What did you say just now?
☐ 믿을 수가 없어.	It's unbelievable.
	I can't believe it.
	No way.
☐ 내 귀를 믿을 수가 없어.	I can't believe my ears.
	*ears→eyes (눈)
☐ 무슨 일이야?	What's wrong?
	What happened?
☐ 분위기가 왜 이래?	What is going on here?
☐ 세상에! / 하느님 맙소사!	Oh, (my) God!
	Oh, (my) goodness!
	Oh, dear God!

📒 Notes

spooky 소름 끼치는, 섬뜩한　goose bump(s) 소름(=flesh)　close call 아슬아슬한 순간, 아찔하게 위험한 순간　unexpected 예상치 못한, 갑작스러운　pop-eyed 눈이 휘둥그레진　go on 〈진행〉 ~이 일어나다

12 창피, 당황스러움

당황스러울 때 가장 많이 쓰이는 표현은 embarrassed 혹은 embarrassing입니다. 주어가 '사람'인 경우 embarrassed, '사물'인 경우 embarrassing을 쓰면 됩니다. 창피해서 어쩔 줄 몰라 하는 사람에게 Nobody thinks that way.(아무도 그렇게 생각하지 않아. / 너만 그렇게 생각하는 거야.)라고 말해 준다면 훨씬 위로가 되겠죠.

창피해! / 황당해! / 부끄러워!	I'm ashamed. *ashamed = embarrassed, blushed It's embarrassing.
혼란스러워! / 헷갈려!	I'm confused. It's confusing. It confuses me.
어찌할 바를 모르겠어.	I don't know what to do.
얼굴을 들 수가 없어.	I can't hold up my head.
똑바로 쳐다볼 수가 없어.	I can't (even) look at you. I can't (even) look at your eyes.
쥐구멍에라도 들어가고 싶어.	I want to crawl into a mouse hole.
사라져 버리고 싶어.	I want to disappear.
창피해 할 것 없어.	Don't be ashamed.
부끄럽지도 않니?	Aren't you ashamed?
아무도 그렇게 생각하지 않아.	Nobody thinks that way.
누가 생각이나 했겠어?	Who would've thought?

13 귀찮음, 성가심

> 귀찮고 짜증날 때 You're annoying me.(귀찮아.), Stop bothering me.(성가시게 굴지 마.) 하고 상대방에 쏘아 줄 때가 있습니다. 혼자 있고 싶을 때는 Leave me alone.(내버려 둬.)이라고 명확하게 자신의 의사를 전달할 필요가 있죠.

원어민 발음 듣기 ☑☐   회화 훈련 ☐☐   듣기 훈련 ☐☐

□ 귀찮아. / 짜증나.	You're annoying (me).
	You're irritating (me).
	It annoys me.
□ 꺼림칙해.	It bothers me.
	*bother = bug
	It's bothering me.
□ 성가시게 굴지 마.	Stop bothering me.
	Don't bother me.
	Get off my back.
□ (짜증스럽게) 또 뭐야.	Now what?
□ 날 좀 내버려 둬.	Leave me alone.
	I want to be alone.
□ 상관하지 마.	It's none of your concern.
	*concern = business
	Mind your business.
	Stay out of it.
□ 간섭하지 마.	Don't interrupt me.
	Stop interfering.
□ 꺼져.	Go away.
	Beat it.

	Get lost.
	Buzz off.
내 사생활이야.	It's my privacy.
이래라저래라 하지 마.	Don't tell me what to do.
	Don't try to control me.
	Don't say "do this or do that."
	Don't push me around.
	*push = boss
내 일은 내가 알아서 해.	I can take care of myself.
	I know what I'm doing.
제발 노크해.	Would you please knock?
	Knock first, please.
밤에 전화하지 마.	Don't call me late at night.
(이렇게) 불쑥 찾아오지 마.	Don't burst into my house (like this).
	*burst into = barge in
	Don't show up at my door like this.
잔소리하지 마.	Don't nag at me.
	Stop giving me a lecture.
조용히 해.	Just be quiet.
	Stay quiet.
나중에 이야기하자.	Let's talk some other time.
	Can we talk later?

Notes

bother 꺼림칙하다, 고민하게 하다 get off one's back 남을 괴롭히는 일을 그만두다 stay out of ~에 참견하지 않다 interfere 간섭하다 push ~ around ~를 몰아대다, 맘대로 조정하려고 들다(= boss ~ around) burst into 난입하다, 갑자기 뛰어들다(= barge in) show up 모습을 드러내다, 나타나다 nag 잔소리하다

14 그리움

나이가 들수록 예전 생각이 많이 떠오릅니다. 그럴 때 절로 나오는 말이 Good old times!(그때가 좋았지!)나 It brings me back to ~.(옛날 ~ 생각난다.)입니다. 보고 싶은 사람이 있으면 I miss her.(보고 싶어.)이나 I'm dying to see her.(보고 싶어 미치겠어.)와 같은 말도 하게 되죠.

원어민 발음 듣기 ☑□ 회화 훈련 □□ 듣기 훈련 □□

□ 옛날이(그때가) 좋았는데. Good old times!
 Those were the times!

□ 행복한 날들이었어. (They were) Happy days.

□ 십대 때 생각이 나게 하는구나. It brings me back to my teens.
 It reminds me of my teens.

□ 시간을 되돌릴 수 있다면. I wish I could turn the clock back.

□ 네가 (너무) 보고 싶어. I miss you (so much).

□ 네가 보고 싶어 죽겠어. I'm dying to see you.

□ 그녀는 많이 변했겠지. She must have changed a lot.

□ 우린 그곳에 가곤 했어. We used to go there.

□ (전에) 여기 와 본 적이 있어. I have been here (before).

□ 첫 직장이었지. It was my first job.

□ 누구나 처음은 잊지 못해. We all remember our first.

□ 어디서 본 듯해. It looks very familiar to me.
 It's déjàvu all over again.

Notes

remind A of B A에게 B를 연상시키다, 생각나게 하다   turn back ~을 되돌리다   be dying to ~ ~하고 싶어 죽겠다   used to 〈과거〉 ~하곤 했다   familiar 익숙한, 친근한

15 걱정, 근심

걱정과 근심이 지나치면 단순히 I'm worried.(걱정돼.)를 넘어 I'm sick to worry.(걱정돼 미치겠어.), I couldn't sleep a wink.(한숨도 못 잤어.)와 같은 말을 하곤 합니다. 그럴 때 Don't worry.(걱정 마.)나 You're not alone.(넌 혼자가 아니야.) 등의 말로 상대방을 위로해 주면 어떨까요?

원어민 발음 듣기 ☑☐　　회화 훈련 ☐☐　　듣기 훈련 ☐☐

☐ 걱정돼.	I'm worried.
	I'm concerned.
☐ 걱정하지 마.	Don't worry.
	Stop worrying.
	Don't trouble yourself.
☐ 그 사람 괜찮을까?	Is he going to be okay?
☐ 한숨도 못 잤어.	I couldn't sleep a wink.
☐ 무슨 걱정(근심) 있어?	What are you worried about?
	Something troubling you?
☐ 사실은 걱정이 있어.	In fact, I'm in trouble.
☐ 말 못할 고민이야.	I can't tell anyone.
☐ 주변에 도움을 청해.	Get some help.
☐ 조심해!	Watch out!
	Heads up!
	(Be) Careful!
☐ 나중에 후회할 텐데.	You're going to regret this.
	You don't want to do this.

16 의심

어떤 일에 대해 의심이 들 때 It's strange.(뭔가 이상해./의심이 가.)라고도 하고, 비슷한 표현으로 I can smell a rat.(뭔가 수상해./낌새가 이상해.)이라고 말하기도 합니다. 결국 의심이 사실로 드러난다면 나를 속인 상대를 향해 "거짓말쟁이야!", "위선자!"와 같은 말로 비난할 수 있습니다.

원어민 발음 듣기 ☑□   회화 훈련 □□   듣기 훈련 □□

□ 이상해. / 의심이 가.	It's strange. *strange = odd, doubtful It doesn't make (any) sense.
□ 그의 동기가 의심스러워.	I'm suspicious of his motive.
□ 냄새가 나. / 수상해.	I can smell it. I can smell a rat.
□ 그 사람을 신뢰할 수가 없어.	I can't trust him.
□ 그녀가 나를 배신하다니.	How could she betray me?
□ 그녀를 어떻게 믿어?	How could you trust her?
□ 물증이 없어.	There's no (physical) evidence. There's no smoking gun.
□ 나를 시험하는 거야?	Are you testing me? Is this a test?
□ 넌 위선자야!	You have two faces! You're such a hypocrite!
□ 그녀의 의도가 뭘까?	What's her intention?
□ 그녀가 정말 원하는 것이 뭘까?	What does she really want?

Chapter 05

대인 관계
Relationship

01 감사 표현   02 축하, 축복   03 칭찬하기   04 양해와 부탁
05 사과와 용서   06 약속   07 손님 초대   08 절친함
09 냉대, 무시   10 반어적, 빈정거리는 표현

감사 표현

감사하는 마음을 전하는 표현할 때 보통 Thank you. 또는 I appreciate it.이라고 합니다. 무엇에 대해 감사하는지를 구체적으로 표현할 때는 Thank you for ~. 혹은 I appreciate ~.와 같이 뒤에 감사의 대상을 말합니다.

원어민 발음 듣기 ☑☐   회화 훈련 ☐☐   듣기 훈련 ☐☐

☐ 매우 감사합니다.	Thank you very much.
	Thanks a lot.
	Thanks a million.
	Many thanks (to you).
	I couldn't thank you enough.
☐ 여러모로 감사합니다.	Thank you for everything.
☐ 어떻게 감사드려야 할지 모르겠어요.	I don't know how to thank you.
☐ 별말씀을요!	No problem!
	No, not at all.
	Don't mention it.
	You're (quite) welcome.
☐ 제가 좋아서 했는데요, 뭐.	It was my pleasure.
	The pleasure is (all) mine.
☐ 감사하다는 말씀 전해 주세요.	Please say many thanks to him for me.
☐ 감사의 표현을 하고 싶어요.	I want to express my appreciation.
☐ 감사의 표시예요.	It's a token of my appreciation.
☐ 이러지 않으셔도 되는데.	You don't have to.
	You shouldn't.

축하, 축복

Congratulations!는 축하할 때 가장 널리 쓰이는 표현입니다. 간단히 Congrats! 라고도 하죠. 무엇을 축하하는지 덧붙이고 싶을 때는 Congratulations on ~ 뒤에 그 내용을 말하면 됩니다. 이때 전치사 on 뒤에는 명사나 동명사만을 쓸 수 있습니다.

원어민 발음 듣기 ☑□　회화 훈련 □□　듣기 훈련 □□

□ 축하해요.	Congratulations! Congrats!
□ 정말 잘됐어요.	(It's) Good for you. (I'm very) Happy for you. (It's) Great to hear.
□ 정말 대견해.	I'm very proud of you. You make me proud. That's my girl.
□ 취업을 축하해요.	Congratulations on your (first) job.
□ 결혼을 축하해요.	Congratulations on your wedding.
□ 승진을 축하해요.	Congratulations on your promotion.
□ 생일을 축하해요.	Happy birthday (to you).
□ 오래오래 사세요.	Have a long healthy life!
□ 늘 건강하세요.	Be healthy. Take good care of yourself.
□ 즐거운 성탄절 보내세요!	Merry Christmas!
□ 즐거운 명절 보내세요!	Happy holidays!

03 칭찬하기

칭찬이 가진 긍정적 효과는 누구나 공감할 것입니다. Good job!(훌륭해!), Keep doing it.(계속 그렇게만 해.) 같은 칭찬의 말을 들으면 누구든지 기분이 으쓱해지고 스스로에 대해 뿌듯함을 느낍니다. 다양한 칭찬의 표현을 알아 두고 많이 사용해 보세요.

원어민 발음 듣기 ✔☐   회화 훈련 ☐☐   듣기 훈련 ☐☐

☐ 잘하고 있어.	(You're) Doing great.
☐ 계속 그렇게(만) 해.	(Just) Keep doing it.
☐ 잘했어. / 훌륭해.	Good job!
	Great work!
	Nicely done!
	Well done!
☐ 최고야.	You're the best.
☐ 그에 대한 칭찬이 자자해.	Everybody praises him.
	Everyone speaks highly of him.
☐ 그는 칭찬받을 만해.	He deserves praise.
☐ 그는 믿음직해.	He is reliable.
	He is trustworthy.
☐ 그의 말에는 무게가 있어.	His words have weight.
☐ 그녀는 경험이 많아.	She has many experiences.
☐ 그녀는 세상사를 잘 알아.	She knows the world.
	She has been around.
☐ 그녀는 인맥이 넓어.	She has many connections.
	She has many strings to pull.

▢ 그녀는 매너가 좋아.	She is well-mannered.
	She has excellent manners.
	*manners = etiquettes
	She always acts properly.
▢ 그녀는 윗사람에게 예의가 바라.	She respects elders.
	She knows how to treat elders.
▢ 그는 성품이 온화해.	He is sweet and gentle.
	He is a sweet and gentle soul.
▢ 그는 사람들과 잘 어울려.	He makes friends easily.
	He gets along with people.
▢ 모두가 그를 존경해.	Everyone respects him.

📝 Notes

so far 지금까지 keep -ing 계속 ~하다 speak highly of ~를 칭찬하다 deserve ~할 자격이 있다, ~할 만하다 know the world 세상을 알다, 세상 돌아가는 물정을 알다 be around 여기저기 돌아다니다, 경험이 많다, 세상을 잘 알다 connection(s) 인맥, 관계 well-mannered 매너가 좋은, 태도가 올바른 etiquette 에티켓, 예의범절, 매너 get along with ~와 잘 어울리다, 금방 친구가 되다

04 양해와 부탁

앞사람이 천천히 걷거나 길을 막고 있을 때 말없이 좁은 틈을 비집고 지나가기보다는 Excuse me.(실례합니다.) 또는 Can I get by?(지나가도 될까요?)라고 한마디 하는 것이 상대방의 기분을 상하게 하지 않을 겁니다. 양해를 구하거나 부탁하는 표현에는 어떤 것이 있는지 알아보겠습니다.

실례지만, ~ / 죄송하지만, ~	Excuse me, but… *excuse = pardon I'm sorry, but…
금방 돌아올게요.	I'll be right back.
잠깐만 기다려 주세요.	Give me one second. Could you wait for a second? Mind if you wait for a second?
그를 잠깐 빌려도 될까요?	Can I borrow him for a second? I need him for a second.
(길에서) 지나갈게요.	Excuse me. Can I get by? Passing through.
문 좀 잡아 주세요.	Hold the door, please.
부탁해도 될까요?	Can I ask you a favor? Could you do me a favor?
무리한 부탁인 줄 압니다만, ~	I know it's too much, but…
간청할게요.	I'm begging you.

MP3를 들어보세요 05-U05

05 사과와 용서

"~해서 미안해."라는 표현은 I'm sorry for ~. 혹은 I'm sorry that ~.의 형태로 씁니다. 용서를 구할 때는 Please forgive me.(용서해 줘.) 혹은 Please accept my apology.(내 사과를 받아 줘.)라고 말하죠. '화해하다'라는 의미로 자주 쓰이는 표현인 make up도 같이 기억해 두세요.

원어민 발음 듣기 ☑☐   회화 훈련 ☐☐   듣기 훈련 ☐☐

☐ 정말 미안해.
I'm so sorry.
*so = very, really, terribly, deeply
I owe you an apology.

☐ ~해서 미안해.
I'm sorry for…
I'm sorry that…

☐ 내가 얼마나 미안한지 넌 모를 거야.   You have no idea how sorry I am.

☐ 내가 제정신이 아니었나 봐.
I must have gone crazy.
I must have been mad.
I must have been out of my mind.

☐ 그땐 나도 내가 아니었어.
I wasn't myself then.

☐ 요즘 내가 내가 아니야.
I haven't been myself lately.

☐ 마음 상하게 할 생각은 없었어.
I didn't mean to hurt you.
I didn't mean to hurt your feelings.
Hurting you is the last thing I would do.

☐ 나도 내가 왜 그랬는지 몰라.
I don't know why I did that.

☐ 내가 지나쳤어.
I was too much.
I went too far.

☐ 용서해 줘.
Please forgive me.

	Please accept my apology.
□ 깨끗이 잊어 줘.	Please forget it.
	Please forget everything.
□ 용서해 주기를 바라지도 못하겠어.	I don't expect you to forgive me.
□ 다시는 이런 일 없을 거야.	It won't happen again.
□ 맹세해.	I swear (to God).
	Cross my heart.
□ 우리 화해하자.	Let's make up.
	Let's drop it.
	Why don't we let it go?
□ 내가 보상할게.	I'll make it up for you.
□ 방해해서 미안해.	(I'm) Sorry to interrupt.
	*interrupt = interfere
□ 갑자기 전화해서 미안해.	(I'm) Sorry to call you out of the blue.
	Sorry to call you suddenly.
□ 걱정을 끼쳐 죄송합니다.	(I'm) Sorry to make you worry.
□ 부담 드려 죄송합니다.	(I'm) Sorry to be a burden.
□ 나한테 사과해.	You owe me an apology.
□ 그걸 지금 사과라고 하는 거야?	Is that an apology?

📋 Notes

be out of one's mind 제정신이 아니다, 정신 나가다 the last thing 절대 하지 않을 것, 절대 하고 싶지 않는 일 go too far 지나치다, 과하다 swear 맹세하다 cross one's heart 맹세하다, 약속하다 make up 화해하다 make it up for ~ ~에게 보상하다 interfere 간섭하다 be out of the blue 난데없이, 갑작스럽게 burden 짐, 부담

약속

일반적으로 '약속하다'라는 의미로 쓰이는 동사는 promise입니다. 그러나 친구들과의 만남 같이 '계획'을 의미하는 약속이라면 plan을 쓰는 것이 더 알맞습니다. '저녁 약속'이나 '저녁 회식'은 dinner plan이라고 쓰면 됩니다.

원어민 발음 듣기 ☑☐   회화 훈련 ☐☐   듣기 훈련 ☐☐

☐ 약속해.	Promise me.
☐ 약속할게.	I promise you.
	I'll promise.
	You have my word.
☐ 한 가지만은 약속할 수 있어.	I can promise you one thing.
☐ 약속은 지켜야지.	You should keep promises.
☐ 약속이 있어.	I have a plan.
	I have an appointment.
	*appointment는 '병원 예약'이나 '업무 관련 약속'을 가리킬 때 주로 쓴다.
☐ 선약이 있어.	I've already made a plan.
	I already have a plan.
	I have a previous appointment.
☐ 일주일 전에 한 약속이야.	The plan was made a week ago.
	*made = set
☐ 지금 와서 취소할 수 없어.	I can't cancel it now.
	It must be rude to cancel it now.
☐ 시간 있어?	Do you have time?
☐ 언제 어디서 만날까?	When and where should we meet?

☐ 7시에 신촌에서 만날까?	How about Sinchon at 7?
	Let's meet around Sinchon at 7.
☐ 시간(장소)를 바꿔도 될까?	Can we change the time(place)?
	*change = switch
	Mind if I change the time(place)?
☐ 10분 늦을 것 같아.	I'm going to be there 10 minutes late.
☐ 무슨 일 있으면 전화 줘.	Call me when something's up.
☐ 늦으면 전화해.	Call me when you are late.
☐ 나 좀 일찍 도착했어.	I came a little early.
	I got here a bit early.
☐ 늦어서 미안해.	I'm sorry I'm late.
	I'm sorry to have kept you waiting.
☐ 나 바람맞았어.	I was stood up.
☐ 기다릴게.	I'll wait for you.
	I'll be waiting for you.
☐ 천천히 와.	Take your time.
	You don't need to be in a hurry.

📋 Notes

have one's word 약속하다　appointment 〈격식〉 약속　previous 사전의, 이전의　set 정하다, 확정하다　rude 무례한, 불손한　switch 바꾸다, 전환하다　something's up 어떤 일이 생기다　be stood up 바람맞다　be in a hurry 급하다, 서두르다

07 손님 초대

상대방을 집 등에 초대할 때는 Would you like to come? 또는 I'd like to invite you to ~.라고 말합니다. 편한 사이라면 간단하게 Want to join us? 또는 Come and visit us.라고 말하기도 하죠. 초대를 받고 온 손님에게는 Make yourself at home.(내 집처럼 편히 계세요.)이라고 말하는 것도 잊지 마세요.

오실래요?	Would you like to come?
	Want to join us?
	Come and visit us.
꼭 오셔야 해요.	You have to come.
와 주시면 영광입니다.	It would be a great honor to have you.
	It would be a great honor if you come.
초대해 주셔서 감사합니다.	Thank you for inviting me.
와 주셔서 감사합니다.	Thank you for coming.
언제든지 환영합니다.	You're always welcome.
	You're welcome anytime.
집들이 오실래요?	Would you like to come to our housewarming party?
몸만 와.	Just bring yourself.
옷 주세요.	Let me get your jacket.
앉으세요.	Please have a seat.
내 집처럼 편히 계세요.	Make yourself at home.
	Make yourself comfortable.

08 절친함

가까운 사이라는 의미로 "우리 친해요."는 We're close.라고 표현합니다. 친한 친구임을 나타낼 때는 He is my best friend., We went to school together., We've been friends for 10 years.와 같이 표현할 수 있습니다.

원어민 발음 듣기 ☑☐ 회화 훈련 ☐☐ 듣기 훈련 ☐☐

□ 우린 (아주) 친해. 가까워.	We are (very) close.
□ 그는 나의 가장 친한 친구야.	He is my best friend.
□ 너희는 얼마 동안 친구였어?	How long have you been friends?
□ 우린 오랜 친구야.	We've been friends for years. It's been many years.
□ 고등학교 이후로 계속 친구야.	We've known each other since high school. We've been friends since high school.
□ 우리는 학교를 같이 다녔어.	We went to school together.
□ 우리는 뗄 수 없는 사이지.	We're inseparable. We're soul mates.
□ 그는 (나에게) 거의 가족이야.	He is (like) family (to me).
□ 우린 비밀이 없어.	We don't keep secrets from each other. We don't have any secret.
□ 그녀는 나에 대해 다 알아.	She knows everything about me.
□ 그녀는 항상 내 곁에 있어 줘.	She always stands by me. She is always there for me.

09 냉대, 무시

상대방에게 존중받지 못하는 것만큼 기분 나쁜 일도 없을 겁니다. '냉대하다', 즉 '차갑게 대하다'는 영어로 be cold to someone이라고 합니다. 이 외에도 look down on(~를 깔보다), ignore(무시하다), leave ~ out(~를 따돌리다) 등도 많이 쓰입니다.

원어민 발음 듣기 ☑☐   회화 훈련 ☐☐   듣기 훈련 ☐☐

그들은 나를 냉대해.	They are cold to me.
	They're giving me a cold shoulder.
그들은 나를 무시해.	They're ignoring me.
그는 다른 사람 의견을 무시해.	He ignores other's opinion.
그들은 아는 척도 안 해.	They don't even say "hi" to me.
그들은 나에게 말도 안 해.	They don't even talk to me.
그는 답장이 없어.	He never replies.
	He never writes me back.
그들은 나를 없는 사람 취급해.	They act like I'm not there.
그들은 나를 깔봐.	They look down on me.
	They think I'm an idiot.
	I'm nobody to them.
그들은 나와 눈도 안 마주쳐.	They don't make an eye contact with me.
	They don't even look at my eyes.
그들은 나를 완전히 따돌려.	They leave me entirely out of their conversation.
	I'm completely left out.

10 반어적, 빈정거리는 표현

'잘했다'는 의미의 Nice job!이나 Nice work! 같은 말도 상황에 따라 반어적으로 빈정거리거나 비꼬아 말하는 표현으로 쓰일 수 있습니다. 그러니 칭찬의 말이라도 때와 장소를 잘 가려서 써야 하죠. 말의 억양과 뉘앙스를 잘 살펴서 상대가 칭찬하는 것인지 비꼬는 것인지 구분할 수 있도록 하세요.

그렇게 빈정거리지 마.	Don't be so sarcastic.
그는 항상 빈정거려.	He always makes sarcastic remarks.
그의 빈정거림이 신경에 거슬려.	His sarcasm gets on my nerves.
(빈정거리며) 웃기시네.	(It's) Funny. That is interesting.
계속 말해 봐. 그렇게 되나 보자.	Keep telling yourself.
(빈정거리며) 잘했네!	Nice job!
(빈정거리며) 잘됐네!	Terrific!
(지각한 사람에게) 일찍도 왔네!	You're early!
꼴좋다! / 싸다!	It serves you.
무슨 큰일이라고.	Big deal!
누가 신경 쓴다고.	Who cares?
신경도 안 쓰면서 (쓰는 척하기는).	Like you care.
누가 알겠어?	Who knows?
(비꼬듯이) 너 잘났다!	So you're perfect.
나한테 퍽이나 좋겠네.	How good for me!
(네 뜻대로 해서) 이제 만족해?	You happy now?

Chapter 06

외모
Appearance

01 잘생김, 예쁨   02 못생김   03 개성, 분위기   04 성형, 수술   05 차림새

01 잘생김, 예쁨

MP3를 들어보세요 06-U01

아름다움을 평가하는 기준은 저마다 다르지만 보편적인 기준에서 '잘생긴 외모'와 관련된 표현들을 모았습니다. 남성의 경우 He is full of testosterone.(남성미가 넘쳐.), He's tall.(키가 커.), 여성의 경우는 She is pretty.(예뻐.), She is gorgeous.(아름다워.), She is slim.(날씬해.) 등을 들 수 있겠죠.

원어민 발음 듣기 ☑☐   회화 훈련 ☐☐   듣기 훈련 ☐☐

☐ 그는 잘생겼어.
He's (so) handsome.
He's good-looking.

☐ 그는 정말 멋져.
He's so dreamy.
He's so cool.
He's a hunk.

☐ 그는 남성미가 넘쳐.
He is masculine.
*masculine = manly
He is full of testosterone.

☐ 그는 키가 커.
He is tall.

☐ 키가 얼마나 돼?
How tall are you?
What is your height?
*in centimeters, in inches 같은 길이 단위를 덧붙일 수도 있다.

☐ 그는 체격이 좋아.
He's well-built.
*well-built = well-cut
He has a great frame.
*frame = body
He is an athlete.
He is stout.

☐ 그는 어깨가 딱 벌어졌어.
He has broad shoulders.
He is broad-shouldered.

□ 그는 근육질이야.	He is (very) muscular.
□ 그는 이목구비가 뚜렷해.	He has fine features.
□ 그는 목소리가 좋아.	He has a good voice.
	He has a smooth voice.
□ 그의 걸음걸이가 멋있어.	I like the way he walks.
□ 그녀는 피부가 적당히 탔어.	She looks great tanned.
	She looks good with a tan.
□ 그녀의 검은 피부가 건강해 보여.	She looks healthier with a tan.
□ 그녀는 예쁘게 생겼어.	She is pretty.
	She has a pretty face.
□ 그녀는 아름다워(매력적이야).	She is beautiful.
	*beautiful = attractive
	She is gorgeous.
	She is stunning.
	She is breathtaking.
	She is lovely.
	She is charming.
	She is such a beauty.
□ 그녀는 자연 미인이야.	She is a natural beauty.
□ 그녀는 귀여워.	She is cute.
	She is such a cutie.
	She is as cute as a button.
□ 그녀는 여성미가 넘쳐.	She is feminine.
	*feminine = womanly
□ 그녀는 날씬해. / 몸매가 좋아.	She is slim.
	She is in good shape.
	She looks fit.

□ 넌 어떻게 그렇게 날씬하니?	How do you keep in shape? How do you keep fit?
□ 그녀는 체격이 아담해.	She is small. *small = tiny, petite
□ 그녀는 몸매가 여성스러워.	She has feminine curves. She has a great shape.
□ 그녀는 다리가 길어.	She has long legs.
□ 그녀는 머릿결이 좋아.	She has sleek hair. *sleek = silky
□ 그녀는 머리가 단정해.	Her hair is well-gloomed.
□ 그녀는 긴 생머리야.	She has long and straight hair. Her hair is long and straight.
□ 그녀는 피부가 고와.	She has silky skin. She has soft and smooth skin.
□ 그녀는 피부가 하얘.	She has light skin. *light = fair She is light-skinned. She is fair-skinned.
□ 그녀는 눈이 예뻐.	She has beautiful eyes. *beautiful = gorgeous
□ 그녀는 웃는 얼굴이 예뻐.	She has a great smile. I like the way she smiles. What a smile!

Notes

hunk 멋진 남자 testosterone 테스토스테론(남성 호르몬) frame 몸의 골격 athlete 건장한 체격의 사람 stout 몸이 튼튼한 feature(s) 이목구비, 생김새 be in good shape 몸매가 좋은 keep in shape 몸매를 유지하다 curves 여성의 곡선미

02 못생김

'못생긴', '다리가 짧은', '뚱뚱한'과 같은 표현은 상대적으로 '못생긴' 외모를 묘사하는 말입니다. 특히나 여성들에게 이런 말을 하는 것은 실례일 수 있으니 몸무게나 얼굴에 난 티끌만 한 freckles(주근깨), pimples(여드름)를 지적하는 것도 삼가는 것이 좋겠죠.

원어민 발음 듣기 ☑□   회화 훈련 □□   듣기 훈련 □□

□ 그는 못생겼어.   He isn't good-looking.
   He is ugly.

□ 그는 키가 작아.   He is short.

□ 그는 땅딸막해.   He is nuggetty.
*nuggetty = stumpy

□ 그는 멀대같이 커.   He is lanky.

□ 그녀는 다리가 짧아(허리가 길어).   She has short legs.
   She has a long waist.

□ 그는 어깨가 좁아.   He has narrow shoulders.

□ 그녀는 너무 말랐어.   She is too thin.
*thin = skinny, bony

□ 그녀는 피골이 상접했어.   She is all skin and bones.

□ 그녀는 통통해.   She is chubby.
*chubby = overweight, plump
   She is a bit overweight.

□ 그는 뚱뚱해. / 비만이야.   He is too fat.
   He is overweight.
   He is obese.

□ 그는 이중 턱이야.   He has a double chin.

▫ 그는 뻐드렁니야.	He has buckteeth.
▫ 체중이 얼마나 돼?	How much do you weigh?
	What is your weight?
	*in kilos, in pounds 같은 무게 단위를 덧붙일 수도 있다.
▫ 그는 배가 나왔어.	He has a beer belly.
	He is potbellied.
▫ 그는 대머리야.	He is bald.
	*bald = baldheaded
	He is thin on top.
	He has a receding hairline.
▫ 그녀의 머릿결이 푸석해.	Her hair is very dry.
▫ 그녀의 머리는 부스스해.	Her hair is messy.
▫ 그녀는 머리숱이 적어.	She has thin hair.
	*thin = fine
▫ 그녀의 피부는 거칠어.	She has rough skin.
▫ 그녀의 얼굴은 주근깨투성이야.	Her face is covered with freckles.
▫ 그녀의 얼굴은 여드름투성이야.	Her face is covered with pimples.
▫ 그녀의 얼굴엔 주름이 많아.	Her face is all wrinkled.

📋 Notes

nuggety 키가 작고 뚱뚱한, 땅딸막한(=stumpy) bony 뼈가 앙상한, 여윈 chubby 토실토실한, 포동포동한 overweight 과체중의 obese 뚱뚱한, 살찐, 비만의 beer belly 볼록 튀어나온 배, 술배 potbellied 배가 볼록 튀어나온 thin on top 머리가 빈, 대머리의 messy 엉망인, 지저분한 wrinkled 주름이 많은 thin hair 숱이 적은 머리, 가느다란 머리

03 개성, 분위기

잘생기고 못생긴 것과 상관없이 개성 있는 외모와 분위기를 가진 사람들이 있습니다. 그런 사람들은 double tooth(덧니)나 baldhead(대머리)가 기막히게 잘 어울려 오히려 매력 포인트가 되기도 합니다. 이렇게 외모에서 풍기는 분위기를 나타내는 표현을 살펴보겠습니다.

그녀는 보조개가 귀여워.	She has cute dimples.
그녀는 덧니가 귀여워.	She has a cute double tooth.
그는 대머리가 잘 어울려.	He looks good with a baldhead.
그는 콧수염이 잘 어울려.	He looks good with his mustache.
그는 주걱턱이 그런대로 귀여워.	His spoon-like chin is kind of cute.
그는 잘생긴 편은 아니지만 매력적이야.	He's not handsome but attractive. *handsome = good-looking
그는 지적이야.	He looks intelligent.
그는 부유해 보여.	He looks rich. *rich = wealthy
그녀는 우아해.	She looks elegant. *elegant = graceful
그녀는 중성적이야.	She is an androgynous. She has androgynous features.
그는 무서워 보여.	He looks scary.
그는 후덕해 보여.	He looks generous.
그는 고전적이야.	He looks classic.
그는 도시적이야.	He has an urban image.

그는 촌스러워.	He is rustic.
그녀는 청순가련해 보여.	She looks pure and innocent.
그녀는 얼굴에 개성이 없어.	She has a forgettable face.
그녀는 나이 들어 보여.	She looks old for her age.
그녀는 어려 보여.	She looks young for her age.
그녀는 어떻게 생겼어?	What does she look like?
그의 외모를 묘사해 봐.	Describe what he looks like. Can you describe what he looks like?
그의 모습이 누군가를 떠올리게 해.	He reminds me of someone else.
(~랑 닮았다는) 그런 말 많이 들어.	I get that a lot.
그는 그 영화배우를 꼭 닮았어.	He looks just like that actor. *actor → actress (여자 배우)

Notes

look good with ~이 잘 어울리다   spoon-like 숟가락(주걱) 모양의   androgynous 중성적인, 양성적인   rustic 소박한, 촌스러운, 촌뜨기의   remind A of B A에게 B를 연상시키다

성형 수술

'미용 성형 수술'은 cosmetic plastic surgery라고 합니다. 부위별로 구분하여 '코 수술'은 nose job, 요즘 유행하는 '양악 수술'은 chin job, '주름 제거 수술'은 face-lifts라고 합니다. 성형 수술이나 미용 시술에 대한 표현을 알아봅시다.

원어민 발음 듣기 ☑□　회화 훈련 □□　듣기 훈련 □□

□ (미용) 성형 수술 했어.	I had (cosmetic) plastic surgery. I went through plastic surgery. I got a nip and tuck.
□ 코 수술 했어.	I had a nose job. I had my nose done. *nose job → eyes job (눈 수술)
□ 양악 수술 했어.	I had my chin done.
□ 주름 제거 수술 했어.	I had face-lift.
□ 쌍꺼풀 수술 했어.	I had my double-eyelid done.
□ 보톡스 맞았어.	I got Botox. I got facial Botox injections.
□ 박피했어.	I got facial peeling.
□ 점을 뺐어.	I had moles removed.
□ 지방 흡입 했어.	I had liposuction.
□ 다크서클 제거 수술 했어.	I removed a dark circle on my face.
□ 가슴 확대 수술 했어.	I had breast implants.
□ 그녀는 성형 수술로 아주 달라 보여.	She looks quite different after plastic surgery.

차림새

옷을 잘 입는 사람을 흔히 '패션 감각이 있다'고 표현합니다. 이것을 영어로는 '~에 취향이 고급이다'라는 뜻의 have great taste in ~이나 '~에 안목이 있다'는 의미인 have an eye for ~로 표현합니다. 옷 외에도 화장이나 액세서리, 구두, 가방 등의 소품들에 대해 어떻게 말할 수 있는지 표현들을 알아봅시다.

원어민 발음 듣기 ☑☐   회화 훈련 ☐☐   듣기 훈련 ☐☐

☐ 그는 패션 감각이 있어 (옷을 잘 입어).	He has great taste in fashion. He has an eye for fashion. He has a remarkable sense of fashion. He's trendy. *trendy = fashionable, stylish
☐ 그는 옷을 못 입어.	He has a bad sense of fashion. *a bad 대신 no를 쓰면 "그는 패션 감각이 없어."의 의미이다.
☐ 그는 옷차림이 구식이야.	His fashion is so out of style. His fashion is so outdated.
☐ 그녀는 옷차림이 너무 튀어.	She is dressed too sexually. She wears loud clothes. Her fashion always sticks out.
☐ 그는 옷차림이 수수해.	He is dressed simply. He wears comfortable clothes.
☐ 그는 옷차림이 단정해.	He's dressed neat and tidy. He's neatly dressed.
☐ 그는 정장 차림을 좋아해.	He likes to dress up. He always suits up. He enjoys wearing suits.

□ 그는 캐주얼 차림을 좋아해.	He likes casual clothes. *like = wear He enjoys wearing casual clothes.
□ 그녀는 화장을 잘해.	She puts on make-up well. *put on = wear She looks great in make-up.
□ 그녀는 화장이 자연스러워.	She wears light make-up and looks natural.
□ 그녀는 화장을 못해.	She's not good at wearing make-up.
□ 그녀는 화장이 너무 진해.	She puts on thick make-up. *thick = heavy, too much
□ 그녀는 액세서리를 잘 해.	She looks great with (fashion) accessories.
□ 그녀는 액세서리 잘 할 줄 몰라.	She doesn't know how to wear accessories.
□ 그녀는 큰 가방이 잘 어울려.	She looks great with a big bag.
□ 그녀는 하이힐이 잘 어울려.	She looks great in high heels.
□ 그는 최신 유행을 따라.	He follows the latest fashion. *fashion = trends He takes fashion trends seriously.
□ 난 유행에 신경 쓰지 않아.	I don't follow the latest fashion.
□ 내 나름의 패션 스타일이 있어.	I have my own fashion style. I like the way I dress.
□ 난 색깔을 잘 맞춰.	I try to match the colors of my clothes.

Notes

a sense of fashion 패션 감각   be out of style 유행이 뒤떨어지다, 구식이다   outdated 구식의   stick out 두드러지다, 튀다   neat and tidy 깔끔하고 단정한   latest 최신의

Chapter 07

성격
Personality

01 개혁적인 성격　02 다정다감한 성격　03 성공 지향적인 성격　04 낭만적인 성격
05 지적인 타입　06 성실, 안정적인 성격　07 열정적인 성격　08 솔직하고 과감한 성격
09 외유내강인 성격　10 기타

개혁적인 성격

애니어그램(enneagram)에서 나누는 아홉 가지 인간의 성격 유형에 대한 표현들을 배워 보겠습니다. Reformer(개혁가)로 알려진 1번 유형은 목표가 뚜렷한 a man of principle(원칙주의자)로 self-control(자기 절제)을 잘하고 perfection(완벽주의)을 추구하는 사람입니다.

원어민 발음 듣기 ☑☐   회화 훈련 ☐☐   듣기 훈련 ☐☐

☐ 그녀는 인내심이 있어.   She is patient.

☐ 그녀는 항상 노력해.   She always tries hard.

☐ 그녀는 절대 포기하지 않아.   She never gives up in the middle.
She does her best.

☐ 그는 옳고 그름을 잘 따져.   He always tells what is right and wrong.

☐ 그는 개혁적이야.   He wants to try new things.
He wants to change things.

☐ 그는 원칙주의자야.   He is a man of principle.
He wants to follow principles.
He thinks rules are very important.

☐ 그녀는 목표가 뚜렷해.   She has a clear goal.
She has a clear sense of purpose.

☐ 그녀는 자기 절제를 잘 해.   She is self-controlled.
*self-controlled = moderate

☐ 그녀는 완벽주의야.   She is a perfectionist.
She wants to be perfect.

☐ 그는 카리스마가 있어.   He is charismatic.
He has charisma.

02 다정다감한 성격

MP3를 들어보세요 07-U02

Helper(조력가)로 알려진 2번 유형의 사람은 warm-hearted(다정다감)하고 social(사교적인)한 성격의 소유자로 남을 돕는 것을 무척 좋아합니다. 늘 energetic(에너지가 넘치는) 해서 여러 사람들과 다양한 관계 맺기를 즐기는 사람이죠. 남을 기쁘게 하는 데서 true meaning of life(진정한 삶의 의미)를 찾는다고 합니다.

원어민 발음 듣기 ☑☐   회화 훈련 ☐☐   듣기 훈련 ☐☐

☐ 그녀는 남을 도와주는 걸 좋아해.	She likes to help other people.
	She feels good when she helps people.
☐ 그녀는 사교적이야.	She is social.
	She is quite a social person.
☐ 그녀는 활동적이야.	She is proactive.
	She is a dynamic person.
☐ 그녀는 에너지가 넘쳐.	She is energetic.
	She is filled with energy.
☐ 그녀는 이타적이야.	She is altruistic.
	She puts other people before herself.
☐ 그는 사려 깊어.	He is considerate.
	*considerate = thoughtful
☐ 그는 사람을 좋아해.	He likes people.
	He is a people person.
☐ 그는 다정다감해.	He is sweet.
	He is such a sweetheart.
	He is warm-hearted.
☐ 그는 다른 사람의 의견을 존중해.	He respects other people's opinions.

03 성공 지향적인 성격

MP3를 들어보세요 07-U03

Achiever(성공 지향적 인물)인 3번 유형은 progressive(진취적)하고 성취욕이 강합니다. 어떤 일이든 달려들어 성공시키려고 애쓰는 active doer(도전적이고 실천적인 인물)라고 할 수 있죠. 하지만 지나치게 성공에 집착한다면 workaholic(일 중독자)이 되거나 full of vanity(허영)에 빠질 수도 있습니다.

원어민 발음 듣기 ☑☐　　회화 훈련 ☐☐　　듣기 훈련 ☐☐

☐ 그는 진취적이야.	He is progressive. *progressive = aggressive
☐ 그는 성취욕이 강해.	He wants to feel a sense of achievement. He looks for something very fulfilling.
☐ 그는 성공 지향적이야.	Success in life is very important to him. He always pursues success.
☐ 그는 화술이 뛰어나.	He has excellent verbal skills.
☐ 그녀는 적응력이 뛰어나.	She is highly adaptable.
☐ 그녀는 경쟁심이 강해.	She is competitive.
☐ 그녀는 질투심이 강해.	She is a jealous type.
☐ 그녀는 실천적이야.	She is a doer. She acts first.
☐ 그는 추진력이 있어.	He has the drive. He is a real go-getter.
☐ 그는 허영이 심해.	He is full of vanity.
☐ 그는 일 중독자 같아.	He can be a workaholic. He has no (personal) life.

04 낭만적인 성격

4번 유형의 사람은 전형적인 낭만주의자입니다. 개인의 감정에만 신경 쓰는 경향이 있기 때문에 흔히 이들을 Individualist(개인주의자)라고 하죠. 하지만 artistic(예술적인) 한 기질이나 천부적인 심미안을 갖고 있어 예술계에서 활동하기에 적합하다고 합니다.

원어민 발음 듣기 ☑☐   회화 훈련 ☐☐   듣기 훈련 ☐☐

☐ 그는 낭만적이야.	He is romantic.
	He is romantic with a capital R.
	He likes to do something romantic.
☐ 그는 명상을 즐겨.	He enjoys meditating. *meditating = contemplating
☐ 그녀는 창조적이야.	She is creative.
	She has a creative mind.
☐ 그는 직관력이 뛰어나.	He is highly intuitive. *intuitive = perceptive
☐ 그는 심미안이 있어.	He has an eye for beauty.
☐ 그녀는 예술가적 기질이 있어.	She is artistic.
☐ 그녀는 감상적이야.	She is quite sentimental.
	She is melodramatic.
☐ 그녀는 매사에 예민해.	She is sensitive.
☐ 그는 감수성이 예민해.	He is impressionable.
☐ 그는 쉽게 상처 받아.	He gets easily hurt by people.
☐ 그녀는 비현실적이야.	She is unrealistic. *unrealistic = impractical
☐ 그녀는 즉흥적이야.	She is whimsical.

05 지적인 타입

Investigator(조사자)란 별명답게 지적 탐구심이 강합니다. 이들은 logical (논리적인)하고 rational(이성적인)하여 객관적으로 판단하기를 좋아하고 스스로를 공명정대한 사람이라고 인식할 때 만족감을 느낀다고 하죠. 또한 새로운 것에 대한 호기심이 강하고 두뇌 활동을 좋아하기 때문에 배움에 대한 열정이 강하다고 합니다.

원어민 발음 듣기 ☑☐   회화 훈련 ☐☐   듣기 훈련 ☐☐

그는 지적이야.	He is intellectual.
그는 논리적이야.	He is logical. He is a logical thinker.
그는 이성적이야.	He is rational.
그는 객관적이야.	He is objective.
그녀는 공명정대해.	She is fair. *fair = impartial She doesn't take any sides.
그녀는 머리 쓰기를 좋아해.	She likes to use her head. *head = brain She likes to challenge her brain.
그는 배우는 것을 좋아해.	He likes learning. He likes to learn new things.
그는 책임감이 강해.	He is responsible.
그녀는 (항상) 침착해.	She is calm and composed. She (always) stays cool and collected. She is cool-headed.
그녀는 좀처럼 화를 내지 않아.	She doesn't usually lose her temper. She doesn't get angry easily.

06 성실, 안정적인 성격

MP3를 들어보세요 07-U06

Loyalist(충성가)인 6번 유형은 devoted(헌신적인)하며 성실한 타입입니다. 사회 전체가 원활하게 제 기능을 하게끔 만드는 주역이라고 볼 수 있겠죠. 이 유형의 사람들은 안정 지향적 성향이 강해서 변화보다는 기존의 것을 고수하려고 하며, 불안한 것을 싫어하여 법과 질서를 맹신하는 경향이 있습니다.

원어민 발음 듣기 ☑□　회화 훈련 □□　듣기 훈련 □□

□ 그녀는 성실해.	She is sincere. *sincere = faithful, honest
□ 그녀는 헌신적이야.	She is devoted. *devoted = dedicated She feels comfortable with following orders.
□ 그는 안정 지향적이야.	He tries to keep the balance. He tries to keep things in order. Safety is important to him. He tries everything stable. *stable = settled, steady, balanced
□ 그녀는 누구하고나 잘 어울려.	She gets along with anyone. She makes friends easily.
□ 그는 현실적이야.	He is down-to-earth.
□ 그는 경계심이 많아.	He is precautious. *precautious = wary
□ 그녀는 의심이 많아.	She is skeptical. She is doubting about ~. *about 뒤에는 무엇에 대해 의심이 많은지 대상이 나온다.
□ 그녀는 엄격해.	She is strict.

열정적인 성격

7번 유형은 Enthusiast(열정가)로 매사에 낙관적이고 긍정적인 삶의 태도를 지닌 사람들입니다. 호기심이 대단히 많아 항상 분주히 돌아다니기 때문에 때때로 어린아이처럼 distracted(산만한)하다는 말을 듣기도 합니다. 유머 감각이 풍부하고 짜릿한 흥분과 자극을 즐깁니다.

원어민 발음 듣기 ☑☐　　회화 훈련 ☐☐　　듣기 훈련 ☐☐

☐ 그는 긍정적이야.
He is positive.
*positive = half-full, optimistic, affirmative

☐ 그는 말보다 행동이 앞서.
He is hasty.
He acts rashly.

☐ 그는 앞에 나서기를 좋아해.
He likes people's attention.
He likes to be spotlighted.
*spotlighted = limelighted

☐ 그녀는 호기심이 많아.
She is full of curiosity.
She wants to satisfy her curiosity.

☐ 그녀는 (매우) 열정적이야.
She is (tremendously) passionate.
She is enthusiastic.

☐ 그는 유머 감각이 있어.
He has a sense of humor.

☐ 그는 어린아이 같아.
He acts like a kid.

☐ 그는 항상 분주해.
He is always busy.
He keeps himself busy.

☐ 그녀는 산만해.
She is always distracted.
*distracted = unfocused, inattentive

☐ 그녀는 무모해.
She can be reckless.
*reckless = thoughtless, heady
She does reckless things.

08 솔직하고 과감한 성격

Challenger(도전가)인 8번 유형은 self-confident(자신만만한)하고 의지가 강해서 남으로부터 간섭받는 것을 매우 싫어하고 자기 생각대로 판단하는 스타일입니다. open-hearted(솔직하고)하고 결단력 있으며 타고난 리더십이 있어 사람들을 쉽게 끌어모을 수 있습니다.

원어민 발음 듣기 ☑□   회화 훈련 □□   듣기 훈련 □□

□ 그는 의지가 강해.
He is strong.
He has a strong will.

□ 그녀는 남의 간섭을 매우 싫어해.
She hates interruption.
*interruption = interference

□ 그는 독자적으로 판단해.
He is independent.
He is opinionated.
He has his own idea.

□ 그녀는 자기주장대로 행동해.
She acts independently.
She doesn't listen to anyone.

□ 그녀는 자신만만해.
She is self-confident.
She is full of self-confidence.
She has great faith in herself.

□ 그는 솔직해.
He is honest.
*honest = straight-forward

□ 그는 숨김이 없어.
He is open-hearted.

□ 그녀는 결단력이 있어.
She is decisive.
*decisive = determined

□ 그녀는 리더십이 있어.
She has leadership.

외유내강인 성격

Peacemaker(조정자, 중재자)라는 별칭답게 9번 유형은 성격이 온화해서 긍정적으로 생각하며 항상 모든 것에서 장점을 찾으려는 노력을 게을리하지 않습니다. 자신의 노력으로 화합을 이끌어 냈을 때 가장 큰 기쁨을 느끼지만, 자기주장이 없어 '태평하다', '걱정이 없다', '소극적이다'라는 평가를 받기도 합니다.

원어민 발음 듣기 ☑☐   회화 훈련 ☐☐   듣기 훈련 ☐☐

□ 그는 좋은 쪽으로만 생각해.   He tries to be positive.
　　　　　　　　　　　　　　He looks on the bright side.

□ 그는 온화한 성격이야.   He is gentle.
　　　　　　　　　　　*gentle = quiet, mild

□ 그는 평화를 갈구해.   He longs for peace.

□ 그녀는 외유내강해.   She looks gentle but tough in spirit.
　　　　　　　　　　She is an iron hand in a velvet glove.

□ 그는 자기주장을 하지 않아.   He doesn't usually express his opinion.

□ 그는 남의 의견에 쉽게 동의해.   He easily agrees with others.

□ 그는 걱정이 별로 없어.   He doesn't worry much.
　　　　　　　　　　　　He doesn't have many worries.

□ 그녀는 태평해.   She is easy-going.
　　　　　　　　She has a happy-go-lucky attitude.

□ 그는 소극적이야.   He is passive (in everything).
　　　　　　　　　He is faint-hearted.

□ 그는 현실 도피적이야.   He buries his head in the sand.
　　　　　　　　　　　*buries = hides
　　　　　　　　　　　He can't confront reality.

10 기타

이번에는 성격을 묻는 표현부터 다소 부정적인 성격을 묘사하는 표현들을 살펴보겠습니다. '이기적인', '매사에 부정적인', '교활한', '폭력적인', '덜렁대는', '우유부단한', '고집불통인', '미성숙한' 등은 영어로 뭐라고 할까요?

원어민 발음 듣기 ☑☐   회화 훈련 ☐☐   듣기 훈련 ☐☐

☐ 그녀는 이기적이야.	She is selfish.
☐ 그녀는 영리해.	She is smart. *smart = bright, clever She has the brains.
☐ 그는 아주 명석해.	He is quite brilliant.
☐ 그녀는 현명한 여자야.	She is a wise woman.
☐ 그녀는 부정적이야.	She is pessimistic. *pessimistic = half-empty, gloomy
☐ 그녀는 성숙하지 못해.	She is immature.
☐ 그녀는 고집불통이야.	She is stubborn.
☐ 그는 쌀쌀맞아.	He is cold.
☐ 그는 교활해.	He is cunning. *cunning = manipulative
☐ 그는 성질이 급해.	He is hot-tempered. *hot-tempered = short-tempered He has a hot temper. *hot temper = short temper
☐ 그는 폭력적이야.	He is violent.
☐ 그녀는 덜렁대.	She is clumsy.

□ 그녀는 정리 정돈을 잘해.	She is organized.
□ 그녀는 외향적이야.	She is very outgoing. *outgoing = extrovert
□ 그녀는 내성적이야.	She is an introvert.
□ 그는 개인적인 일은 말 안 해.	He is private.
□ 그는 비밀이 많아.	He has many secrets.
□ 그는 사치스러워.	He is extravagant.
□ 그는 보수적이야.	He's conventional. *conventional = traditional, orthodox
□ 그녀는 충동적이야.	She is impulsive. *impulsive = impetuous
□ 그녀는 엉뚱해.	She is eccentric.
□ 그녀는 미쳤어.	She is a psycho.
□ 그는 수다스러워.	He talks a lot. He is talkative.
□ 그는 말없이 조용해.	He is quiet.
□ 그는 거만해.	He is arrogant. *arrogant = haughty He acts big. He is too proud of himself.
□ 그녀는 겸손해.	She is moderate. *moderate = humble
□ 그는 우유부단해.	He is indecisive. *indecisive = wishy-washy He can't make up his mind easily.
□ 그는 밝고 명랑해.	He is bright and cheerful.

Chapter 08

사랑
Love

01 소개팅에서   02 신상 파악하기   03 데이트 신청하기   04 사랑 고백
05 수락과 거절   06 연애 초기   07 연애 중   08 프러포즈
09 결혼 생활   10 이별할 때

01 소개팅에서

지인의 소개로 만나는 blind date(소개팅)와 관련해서 '~와 소개팅을 시켜 주다'는 set ~ up이라고 표현합니다. 모르는 사람들끼리 만날 수 있도록 setting(주선)을 해 준다는 의미이죠. 소개팅과 관련된 다양한 표현들을 영어로 어떻게 말하는지 알아볼까요?

원어민 발음 듣기 ☑☐ 회화 훈련 ☐☐ 듣기 훈련 ☐☐

□ 소개팅 시켜 줄게.
I'll set you up with someone.
*set = fix
Let me introduce you to someone.

□ 그녀는 내 친구야.
She is my friend.
*friend → colleague from work(직장 동료)

□ (좋은 사람) 소개해 줘.
Set me up with someone (nice).
Fix me up.
Would you introduce me to someone?
Can you set me up on a blind date?

□ 어떤 남자 스타일을 좋아해?
What is your type?
What kind of guys do you like?
*like = prefer
What are you looking for in a guy?

□ 성격 좋은 사람이 좋아.
I like a good-hearted person.
I like someone who has good personality.

□ 잘생긴 사람이 좋아.
I like a good-looking guy.

□ 돈 잘 쓰는 사람이 좋아.
I like a big spender.

□ 같이 나가 줄까?
Do you need a chaperon(e)?
Do you need some help?

□ 소개팅 어땠어?	How was your blind date?
□ 그 여자(소개팅 상대) 어땠어?	What's she like?
□ 그녀가 너무 마음에 들어.	I really like her.
	She is so my type.
	She is the person that I've dreamed about.
□ 그녀는 내게 너무나 과분해.	She is out of my league.
□ 그 사람 괜찮았어.	He is fine.
	He is not so bad.
□ 또 만나기로 했어?	Are you guys going to meet again?
	Are you going to ask her out again?
	Do you have a second date with him?
□ (그다지) 내 타입은 아니야.	She is (so) not my type.
	*so → exactly (not 뒤에 붙인다.)
	She is not my kind of girl.
	She is such a turn-off.
□ (그녀와) 서로 잘 안 맞아.	We don't have chemistry together.
	The chemistry with her isn't right.
□ 그와 더 만나 봐.	Why don't you have another date with him?
	Give him another chance.

📝 Notes

set A up with B A를 B에게 소개시켜 주다(= fix A up with B)   big spender 돈 씀씀이가 큰 사람   chaperon(e) 샤프롱(젊은 여성이 사교계에 나갈 때 도와주는 중년 여성), 남녀가 처음 만날 때 중간에서 도와주는 사람   be out of one's league 과분하다, 상대가 안 되다   ask out 데이트 신청하다   turn-off 지루하게 만드는 것(사람)   chemistry 서로 친해지는 친근감   give ~ a chance ~에게 기회를 주다

02 신상 파악하기

소개팅 자리에서 만난 사람들이 서로에 대한 본격적인 신상 파악에 들어갈 때 age(나이)와 occupation (직업)은 물론 family(가족), hobby(취미), school(학교), major(전공) 등에 대한 다양한 이야기를 나누죠. 하지만 초면에 너무 무례하거나 실례가 되는 질문은 자제하는 것이 좋습니다.

원어민 발음 듣기 ☑☐   회화 훈련 ☐☐   듣기 훈련 ☐☐

□ 궁금한 거 물어보세요.   Ask anything about me.

□ 저한테 궁금한 거 없으세요?   Aren't you curious about me?

□ 나이는 몇 살이에요?   How old are you?
　　　　　　　　　　　May I ask how old you are?
　　　　　　　　　　　What is your age?

□ 저와 동갑이네요.   We're both of same age.

□ 저보다 세 살 위네요.   You're three years older than me.

□ 저보다 세 살 아래네요.   You're three years younger than me.

□ 몇 살 같아 보여요?   How old do I look?
　　　　　　　　　　Can you guess my age?

□ 직업은 뭐예요?   What do you do (for a living)?
　　　　　　　　What's your profession?
　　　　　　　　What's your occupation?
　　　　　　　　What line of business are you in?

□ 일은 마음에 들어요?   Do you like your job?
　　　　　　　　　　*job = work
　　　　　　　　　　Are you satisfied with your work?

□ 가족은 어떻게 되나요?   How big is your family?

□ 형제는 어떻게 되나요?	Do you have any siblings?
□ 취미는 무엇인가요?	What's your hobby?
	What do you usually do when you are free?
□ 소개팅 자주 하나요?	Are you on a blind date a lot?
□ 주말엔 주로 뭐하나요?	What do you do on the weekend?
□ 어떤 공부했어요?	What did you study?
	What was your major?
□ 종교는 뭐예요?	What's your religion?
□ 요즘은 어떤 것에 관심 있나요?	What interests you these days?
	What are you interested in these days?

Notes

profession 직업(= occupation)　　be interested in ~에 관심이 있다

03 데이트 신청하기

MP3를 들어보세요 08-U03

상대방이 마음에 들어 데이트 신청을 할 때 가장 흔하게 쓰는 표현은 Would you like a coffee with me?(커피 한잔 할래요?)나 Would you like to have dinner with me?(저녁 같이 할래요?)입니다. 꼭 커피나 식사에 관심이 있다기보다는 그 시간 동안 서로에 대해 알아가고 좀 더 발전된 관계를 원한다는 의미입니다.

원어민 발음 듣기 ☑□   회화 훈련 □□   듣기 훈련 □□

□ 데이트 신청할게요.	I'd like to ask you out.
□ 저랑 데이트할래요?	Do you want to go out with me?
	Would you go on a date with me?
□ 이번 주말에 시간 있어요?	What are you doing this weekend?
	Are you free this weekend?
□ 사귀는 사람 있어요?	Are you seeing someone?
	Do you have a boyfriend?
□ 나 어떻게 생각해요?	What do you think about me?
	What do you think of me as your girlfriend?
□ 커피 한잔 할래요?	Would you like a (cup of) coffee with me?
□ 저녁 같이 할래요?	Would you like to have dinner with me?
	Do you want to have dinner with me?
□ 술 한잔 할래요?	Can I buy you a drink?
□ 영화 보러 갈래요?	Do you want to see a movie with me?
□ 드라이브 갈래요?	Do you want to go for a ride?

사랑 고백

사랑을 고백하는 표현은 매우 다양합니다. 흔하게는 I love you.(사랑해.)에서부터 I'm in love with you.(사랑에 빠졌어.), I'm crazy about you.(너에게 미쳐 있어.), I can't live without you.(너 없이 못살아.), I've never felt this way before.(이런 느낌 처음이야.)와 같이 강한 표현들도 있습니다.

원어민 발음 듣기 ☑□   회화 훈련 □□   듣기 훈련 □□

□ 사랑해. / 사랑에 빠졌어.	I love you. I'm in love with you. I'm falling in love with you.
□ 넌 내 마음을 훔쳐 갔어.	You stole my heart.
□ 내 마음 전부를 주고 싶어.	I want to give you my whole heart.
□ 홀딱 반했어.	I have a huge crush on him. *huge = major I have the biggest crush on her.
□ 첫눈에 반했어.	It was love at first sight. We clicked right away. I just knew she was the one.
□ 널 사랑하는 것 같아.	I think I'm in love with you.
□ 그를 좋아하는 것 같아.	I have feelings for him. I think I like him.
□ 그녀에게 끌려.	I'm attracted to her.
□ 이런 느낌 처음이야.	I've never felt this (way) before. It's the first time to feel this way.
□ 네가 염려돼.	I care about you.

☐ 너한테 미쳐 있어.	I'm crazy about you.
☐ 난 너 없이 못 살아.	I can't live without you. *live = survive, breathe
☐ 너는 내게 전부야.	You're everything to me. You're the world to me.
☐ 네가 늘 보고 싶어.	I miss you all the time.
☐ 요즘 네 생각만 해.	You're all I think about lately. I think about you all the time.
☐ 너에 대해 모든 것을 알고 싶어.	I want to get to know all about you.
☐ 우린 잘 어울리는 한 쌍이야.	We belong together.
☐ 혼자인 건 정말 싫어.	I hate being single.
☐ 네 남자 친구가 되고 싶어.	I want to be your boyfriend.
☐ 내 인생에 여자는 너뿐이야.	You're the woman of my life.
☐ 너처럼 아름다운 여자는 처음 봤어.	You're the most beautiful girl I've ever seen.

📝 Notes

be in love with ~와 사랑에 빠지다(= fall in love with)　**have a crush on** ~에게 반하다　**click** 서로 잘 통하다　**right away** 바로, 단번에　**feelings** 감정, 느낌　**be attracted to** ~에게 끌리다, 매력을 느끼다　**get to know** 알게 되다, 친해지다　**belong** ~에게 속하다

05 수락과 거절

상대방의 사랑 고백을 받아들일 때 I love you, too.(나도 널 사랑해.) 혹은 Let's date.(우리 사귀자.)와 같은 표현을 쓸 수 있습니다. 거절할 때는 I like you, but I don't love you.(널 좋아하지만 사랑하지는 않아.), You're a great person, but… (넌 좋은 사람이지만……)과 같은 말로 얼버무리기도 합니다.

원어민 발음 듣기 ☑□   회화 훈련 □□   듣기 훈련 □□

□ 나도 널 사랑해.
I love you, too.
I'm in love with you, too.

□ 언제 고백하나 기다렸어.
I thought you never ask me out.

□ 생각해 볼게.
Give me some time to think about it.

□ 너한테 관심 없어.
I'm not interested in you.
I don't feel anything for you.

□ 널 좋아하지 않아.
I don't like you.

□ 널 이성으로 여기지 않아.
You're just my friend, nothing more.
I don't feel the same way you feel about me.

□ 몇 번 잔 것뿐이잖아.
We slept together a few times.
We just hooked up a couple of times.

□ 서로 즐겼을 뿐이잖아.
We were (just) having fun.

□ 친구로 지내자.
Let's be friends.

□ 우린 너무 달라.
We're completely different.
We're total opposite.

□ 헤어진 지 얼마 안 됐어.
I've just got out of long relationship.
I just broke up with someone.

06 연애 초기

> 연애할 때 What shall we do today?(뭐 할까?), Is there a place you want to go?(가고 싶은 데 있어?)라는 말은 일상적으로 쓰고, 집에 데려다 주면서 Don't go.(가지 마.), When can I see you again?(또 언제 만나?)와 같은 말도 자주 하죠. 이러한 표현들을 영어로는 어떻게 하면 되는지 살펴보겠습니다.

원어민 발음 듣기 ☑☐   회화 훈련 ☐☐   듣기 훈련 ☐☐

☐ 오늘 뭐 할까요?
What do you want to do today?
What shall we do today?

☐ 어디 가고 싶어요?
Is there a place you want to go?
Do you want to go somewhere?

☐ 집에 일찍 가야 돼요.
I have to go home early.

☐ 좀 더 같이 있어요.
Stay a little longer.
Can't you stay a little longer?
I'd like to be with you a little longer.

☐ 가지 마세요.
Don't go.
*go = leave

☐ 집에 바래다줄게요.
I'll walk you home.
I'll drive you home.
I'll escort you home.

☐ (집에) 다 왔네요.
We're already here.
This is me.
It's my place.

☐ 오늘 즐거웠어요.
I had a great time today.
*great = wonderful, nice
It was fun today.
Thank you for taking me out today.

☐ 언제 또 만날 수 있어요?	When can I see you again?
	I want to see you again.
☐ 전화해요.	Call me.
☐ 밤에 전화해도 돼요?	Can I call you at night?
☐ 손잡고 싶어요.	I want to hold your hand.
☐ 키스해도 돼요?	Can I kiss you?
	I want to kiss you.
☐ 내 친구들 소개해 줄게요.	I want to introduce my friends to you.
☐ 당신을 좋아할 거예요.	They're going to love you.
☐ 만난 지 세 달 정도 됐어요.	We've been going out for about three months.
	We've been seeing each other for over three months.

Notes

walk ~ home ~를 걸어서 집까지 데려다 주다   drive ~ home ~를 차를 태워서 집까지 데려다 주다   escort 에스코트하다, 바래다주다   take ~ out ~를 데리고 나가다   go out 데이트하다, 교제하다

07 연애 중

정식으로 사귀게 되었다면 We're a couple now.(우리 이제 커플이야.) 혹은 We're together now.(우리 이제 사귀어.)라고 말할 수 있습니다. 이때 You look cute together. 하면 "둘이 잘 어울려요."라는 뜻이 됩니다.

원어민 발음 듣기 ☑☐ 회화 훈련 ☐☐ 듣기 훈련 ☐☐

□ 너희 둘 잘 어울려.

You look cute together.
You are a lovely couple.
*lovely = adorable
You are perfect for each other.

□ 너희는 천생연분이야.

You guys are a match made in heaven.
You are meant for each other.
You're made for each other.

□ 둘이 사귀면 잘 어울릴 텐데.

You can make a cute couple.

□ 너희 사귀니?

Are you two dating?
Are you a couple?
Are you seeing each other?

□ 우리 (이제) 사귀어.

We're a couple (now).
We're together (now).
We're dating.

□ 둘이 어떻게 만났어?

How did you (two) meet?

□ 데이트한 지 얼마나 됐어?

How long have you been going out?
How long have you been seeing her?

☐ 1년 됐어.	It's been a year.
☐ 만났다 헤어졌다 한 지 2년 됐어.	On and off for two years.
☐ 사귄 지 오래됐어.	We've been seeing each other for a long time.
☐ 우린 결혼한 노부부 같아.	I feel like we're an old married couple.
☐ 우리 처음으로 싸웠어.	We had our first fight.
☐ 무엇 때문에 싸웠는데?	What did you fight about?
☐ 우린 늘 싸워.	We constantly argue. *argue = fight
☐ 그가 요즘 이상하게 굴어.	He has been acting weird.
☐ 양다리 걸치고 있는 것 같아.	I think he is sitting on the fence.
☐ 바람피우는 것 같아.	I think he is cheating on me.
☐ 그가 진지한 관계를 회피해.	He has a commitment issue. He's terrified by commitment.
☐ 그는 남자 친구 감이 아니야.	He is not boyfriend material. He doesn't know how to be a boyfriend.

📓 Notes

adorable 귀여운, 사랑스러운   match made in heaven 천생연분(= meant for each other)   on and off 했다 안 했다 하는   constantly 지속적으로, 늘   act weird 이상하게 행동하다   sit on the fence 양다리 걸치다   cheat on ~를 속이다, ~에게 사기 치다, 바람피우다   commitment 진지한 약속, 언약   be terrified by ~에 질겁하다, 공포에 질리다   boyfriend material 남자 친구가 될 만한 자질

프러포즈

청혼의 표현 역시 매우 다양합니다. 간단하게는 Will you marry me?(결혼해 줄래?)부터 조금 더 로맨틱하게 I want to grow old with you.(너와 함께 나이 들고 싶어.), I want to spend the rest of my life with you.(너와 평생 함께 있고 싶어.)와 같은 표현도 있습니다.

원어민 발음 듣기 ☑☐　회화 훈련 ☐☐　듣기 훈련 ☐☐

□ 그녀에게 언제 프러포즈할 거야?　When are you going to propose to her?
*When 대신 How를 쓰면 '어떻게' 청혼할지 방법을 묻는 표현.

□ 반지 샀어?　Did you pick a ring?
*pick = buy

□ 오늘 프러포즈할 거야.　I'm going to propose to her today.
I'm going to pop the question today.

□ 거절하면 어쩌지?　What if she says "No"?

□ 결혼해 줘.　Marry me.
Will you marry me?
*will 대신 would를 쓰면 좀 더 정중한 표현이 된다.

□ 함께 나이 들고 싶어.　I want to grow old with you.

□ 아침에 함께 눈뜨고 싶어.　I want to wake up in the morning together.

□ 너와 늘 함께 있고 싶어.　I want to be with you all the time.
I want to spend the rest of my life with you.

□ 넌 바로 내가 찾던 그 사람이야.　You're the one.

□ 넌 나를 채워 주는 사람이야.　You complete me.

09 결혼 생활

"결혼 생활이 행복해."는 I'm happily married.라고 말합니다. 아이를 가지려고 준비 중일 때는 I want to be a mom.(아이를 가질까 해.)이라고 하죠. 임산부에게 출산일이 언제인지를 물을 때는 When is your due date?라고 합니다.

원어민 발음 듣기 ☑□   회화 훈련 □□   듣기 훈련 □□

□ 우리 막 약혼했어.	We just got engaged.
□ 우리 곧 결혼해.	We're getting married.
□ 날짜는 정했어?	Did you set the wedding date?
□ 결혼식은 언제야?	When is your wedding?
□ 내년 가을이야.	It's next autumn.
□ 결혼 준비는 잘 되어 가?	How's your wedding preparation (going)?
□ 준비할 게 너무 많아.	There are too many things to prepare for the wedding.
□ 우리 막 결혼했어.	We just got married. We're newlyweds.
□ 중매 결혼 했어.	We had an arranged marriage.
□ 연애 결혼 했어.	We had a love marriage.
□ 아직 신혼이야.	We are in our honeymoon.
□ 7년 연애 끝에 결혼했어.	We got married after 7 years dating.
□ 결혼 생활이 행복해.	I'm happily married.
□ 우리 집 샀어.	We've bought a new house.

▫ 아이를 가질까 해.	We're thinking of having a baby. I want to be a mom.
▫ 나 임신했어.	I'm pregnant. I'm going to be a mother. I have a bun in the oven.
▫ 임신 축하해!	Congratulations on becoming a mom!
▫ 출산 예정일이 언제야?	When is your due date? When are you expecting?
▫ 두 달 남았어.	Two more months to go. Two months are left.
▫ 그녀는 쌍둥이 아들을 낳았어.	She gave birth to twin boys.
▫ 아이가 너를 꼭 닮았어.	Your baby looks just like you.
▫ 아이가 네 코를 빼닮았어.	Your baby has got your nose.
▫ 우리 결혼 10주년이야.	It's our 10th wedding anniversary. We've been married for 10 years.
▫ 우리 별거 중이야.	We're separated.
▫ 우리(나) 이혼할 거야.	We're getting divorced. We're falling apart. I'm leaving him.

📝 Notes

newlyweds 신혼부부   have a bun in the oven 임신하다   due date 출산 예정일
expect 출산을 기다리다   give birth 낳다, 출산하다   raise well 잘 키우다   separated 분리된, 부부가 별거 상태인   get divorced 이혼하다   fall apart 산산이 부서지다, 결딴나다

이별할 때

"우리 헤어져."라고 말할 때는 '헤어지다', '결별하다'의 의미인 break up을 써서 Let's break up.이라고 합니다. 이별의 이유로는 We're completely different.(우린 너무 달라.), I've met someone else.(다른 사람이 생겼어.), I don't love you.(너를 사랑하지 않아.) 등이 있겠죠.

원어민 발음 듣기 ☑☐   회화 훈련 ☐☐   듣기 훈련 ☐☐

□ 우리 헤어져.	Let's break up.
	I have to break up with you.
□ 다시는 만나지 말자.	I don't (ever) want to see you again.
□ 전화도 하지 마.	Don't even call me.
□ 너를 (더 이상) 사랑하지 않아.	I don't love you (any more).
□ 우린 너무 달라.	We're completely different.
	We want completely different things.
□ 나 다른 사람이 생겼어.	I've met someone else.
	I love someone else.
□ (나에게) 이러지 마.	Please don't do this (to me).
□ 가지 마.	Don't leave me.
□ 내가 뭘 잘못했어?	What did I do wrong?
	Tell me what I've done.
	It's because of me?
□ 다 내 탓이야.	It's because of me.
	It's all my fault.
□ 기회를 줘.	Give me another chance.

앞으로 잘 할게.	I'll do better. *better → different(다른) I'll make it up to you.
우린 끝났어.	We're done. I'm done with you.
더 이상 참을 수 없어.	I can't take him anymore. I'm sick and tired of him.
나 그녀에게 차였어.	I got dumped by my girlfriend. She dumped me.
내가 찼어.	I dumped him.
마음이 (갈가리) 찢어져.	He broke my heart (piece by piece). I'm heart-broken.
그녀를 못 잊겠어.	I can't forget her. I can't get over her. I miss her.
그녀에 대한 사랑을 멈출 수 없어.	I can't stop loving her.
그가 그리울 거야.	I'll miss him.
세상에 남자(여자)는 많아.	There are many other fish in the sea.
그만 정리해.	(It's time to) Move on.

📃 Notes

make it up to ~에게 보상하다   be done with ~과 끝나다, 끝장나다   be sick and tired of ~에 넌더리가 나다   get dumped 차이다   dump ~를 차다   heart-broken 가슴이 찢어지는, 슬픔에 잠긴   get over 어려움을 극복하다, 잊다   other fish in the sea 바다의 다른 물고기(교제할 상대가 많다는 의미)   move on 지난 것을 정리하고 새것으로 옮겨가다, 새 출발하다

Chapter 09

하루 일과
Daily routine

01 평일 오전　**02** 평일 오후, 저녁　**03** 주말　**04** 명절, 국경일, 기념일

01 평일 오전

weekdays(평일) 오전은 대부분 출근이나 등교 준비로 바쁩니다. 씻고, 식사를 하고, 옷을 챙겨 입는 등의 준비를 하죠. 아이가 있다면 책가방 싸기나 과제물 챙기는 것을 도와주고 학교에 바래다주어야 합니다. 집을 나서기 전 문단속하는 것도 빼먹으면 안 되겠죠. 이런 평일 오전에 하는 일에 대한 표현들을 살펴보겠습니다.

원어민 발음 듣기 ☑☐   회화 훈련 ☐☐   듣기 훈련 ☐☐

☐ 아침에 일어납니다.	I get up in the morning. *get up = wake up
☐ 하품을 합니다.	I yawn.
☐ 기지개를 켭니다.	I stretch myself.
☐ 침대를 정돈합니다.	I make my bed.
☐ 조깅을 합니다.	I jog.
☐ 양치질을 합니다.	I brush my teeth.
☐ 세수를 합니다.	I wash my face.
☐ 샤워를 합니다.	I take a shower.
☐ 머리를 감습니다.	I wash my hair. I shampoo my hair.
☐ 머리를 빗습니다(손질합니다).	I comb my hair. *comb = brush
☐ 화장을 합니다.	I put on some make-up.
☐ 모닝커피를 마십니다.	I have morning coffee.
☐ 아침 식사를 합니다.	I have breakfast. *have 대신 skip을 쓰면 "아침 식사를 거르다"의 의미이다.

☐ 신문을 봅니다.	I read the newspaper.
☐ 라디오를 듣습니다.	I listen to the radio.
☐ 용변을 봅니다.	I go to the bathroom. I use the toilet.
☐ 옷을 갈아입습니다.	I get dressed. I change my clothes.
☐ 교복을 입습니다.	I put on my school uniform.
☐ 넥타이를 맵니다.	I wear a tie.
☐ 신발을 신습니다.	I put on shoes.
☐ 아이들을 깨웁니다.	I wake my kids up.
☐ 아이의 옷을 입힙니다.	I get my kids dressed.
☐ 아이 가방 싸는 것을 챙겨 줍니다.	I help my kids pack the school bag.
☐ 가스를 점검합니다.	I check the gas stove turned-off. *gas stove → room light(전등)
☐ 문단속을 합니다.	I check the door locked.
☐ 아이를 학교에 바래다줍니다.	I take my kids to school.
☐ 출근을 합니다.	I go to work. *go to work = go to the office I leave for work.
☐ 학교에 갑니다.	I go to school.
☐ 도서관에 갑니다.	I go to the library.

📝 Notes

put on 입다, 쓰다, 걸치다   skip 건너뛰다, 뛰어넘다   get dressed 옷을 입다   pack the bag 가방을 싸다   gas stove 가스레인지   lock 잠그다, 닫아걸다   leave for ~하러 떠나다

02 평일 오후, 저녁

평일 오후와 저녁에는 학교 수업이나 업무를 마치고 귀가하기, 저녁 식사 등의 활동이 이루어집니다. 잠자리에 들기까지 TV를 시청하거나 가족들과 담소를 나누기도 하죠. 자기 전에 알람 시계를 맞춰 놓는 일도 잊지 마세요.

원어민 발음 듣기 ☑□   회화 훈련 □□   듣기 훈련 □□

□ 아이를 학교에서 데려옵니다.   I pick my kids up from school.

□ 식료품을 사러 갑니다.   I go to the grocery store.

□ 간식거리를 삽니다.   I get some snacks.

□ 귀가합니다.   I come (back) home.

□ 저녁을 차립니다.   I cook dinner.
                                 I fix a meal.

□ 저녁 식사를 합니다.   I have dinner.

□ 식탁을 치웁니다.   I clean up the kitchen table.

□ 설거지를 합니다.   I wash the dishes.
                                 *wash = clean

□ TV를 시청합니다.   I watch TV.

□ 가족들과 담소를 나눕니다.   I chat with my family.

□ 아이 잠자리를 봐 줍니다.   I make a bed for my kids.

□ 아이를 재웁니다.   I put my kids to bed.

□ 잠자리에 듭니다.   I go to bed.
                                 I crawl into bed.
                                 *crawl into = get into

□ 잠이 듭니다.   I fall asleep.

03 주말

꼼짝하기 싫은 weekends(주말)이지만 해야 할 밀린 일들이 많습니다. 집 안 구석구석 청소하기, 빨래하기, 화초에 물 주기, 세탁물 찾기 등이 끝나면 느긋하게 책을 읽거나 음악을 듣기도 하죠. 또한 한 주간 쌓인 스트레스를 풀기 위해 가벼운 운동을 하거나 산책을 즐기는 것도 좋습니다.

원어민 발음 듣기 ☑☐   회화 훈련 ☐☐   듣기 훈련 ☐☐

□ 늦잠을 잡니다.	I get up late. I sleep in. I oversleep.
□ 아침 겸 점심(브런치)을 먹습니다.	I have brunch.
□ 집 안 청소를 합니다.	I clean the house.
□ 욕조를 문질러 닦습니다.	I scrub the bathtub. *bathtub → washstand (세면대)
□ 화초에 물을 줍니다.	I water the plants.
□ 빨래를 합니다.	I do laundry.
□ 빨래를 건조대에 넙니다.	I hang wet clothes.
□ 빨래를 갭니다.	I fold clothes.
□ 재활용 쓰레기를 분리합니다.	I recycle garbage waste.
□ 세탁물 찾습니다.	I pick up my clothes from a (dry) cleaner's.
□ 다림질을 합니다.	I iron.
□ 환기를 시킵니다.	I open the windows to get some fresh air. I open the windows to let some fresh air in.

☐ 영화를 보러 갑니다.	I go to the movies.
☐ 음악을 듣습니다.	I listen to the music.
☐ 독서를 합니다.	I read a book.
☐ 잡지를 뒤적거립니다.	I look through the magazines. *magazines → newspapers(신문)
☐ 쇼핑을 갑니다.	I go shopping.
☐ 외식을 합니다.	I eat out.
☐ 미용실에 갑니다.	I go to the beauty salon. *beauty salon = beauty shop
☐ 머리를 자릅니다.	I get my hair cut. *cut = trimmed
☐ 손톱을 깎습니다.	I clip my nails. *clip = cut, trim
☐ 손톱을 다듬습니다.	I do my fingernails. *do = polish, manicure
☐ 집에서 쉽니다.	I relax at home.
☐ 먹는 것으로 스트레스를 풉니다.	I release stress by eating. *release = ease, get rid of
☐ 컴퓨터 게임을 합니다.	I play computer games.
☐ 낮잠을 잡니다.	I take a nap. I nap. *nap = doze off
☐ 빈둥거립니다.	I loaf around all day long.
☐ DVD를 빌립니다.	I borrow a DVD.
☐ 산책을 합니다.	I take a walk. I go for a walk.

▢ 피크닉을 갑니다.	I go for a picnic.
▢ 운동을 합니다.	I exercise.
	I work out.
▢ 자전거를 탑니다.	I ride a bike.
	*bike = bicycle
▢ 인라인 스케이트를 타러 갑니다.	I go inline-skating.
▢ 교외로 드라이브를 갑니다.	I go for a drive to the suburbs.
▢ 교회(성당)에 갑니다.	I go to church.
▢ 야식을 먹습니다.	I eat late night comfort food.
	I enjoy late night snacks.

Notes

sleep in 늦잠 자다   brunch 브런치, 아침 겸 점심   hang 매달다, 널다   fold 접다, 개다
pick up (사람, 물건 등을) 데려오다, 찾다   look through ~을 통해 보다, 대강 보다   eat out 밖에서 먹다, 외식하다   trim 다듬다   ease 완화하다, 가볍게 하다   doze off 선잠 자다, 졸다
loaf around 빈둥거리다   work out 운동하다   suburb 교외, 대도시 근교

명절, 국경일, 기념일

holidays(명절)에는 가족들이 모두 모여 제사를 지내거나 성묘를 갑니다. 또 전통 음식을 함께 먹고 전통 놀이를 하며 즐거운 시간을 보내기도 하죠. national holidays(국경일)에는 국기를 달고 anniversaries(기념일)에는 축하 파티와 함께 선물을 주고받습니다. 이런 다양한 상황을 영어로는 어떻게 표현할까요?

원어민 발음 듣기 ☑□   회화 훈련 □□   듣기 훈련 □□

□ 고향 부모님 댁에 갑니다.
I visit my parents at home.
I come home.
*come=return

□ 가족과 친척들이 한 자리에 모입니다.
Family and relatives are gathered all together.

□ 근간의 소식을 교환합니다.
We catch up.
We share the news.

□ 성묘를 갑니다.
We go to our family grave.
*go to=visit

□ 벌초를 합니다.
We pull out the weeds around the grave.
*grave=site

□ 국경일에 국기를 답니다.
I fly a flag on a national holiday.

□ 크리스마스트리를 세웁니다.
I set up a Christmas tree.

□ 제야의 종소리를 듣습니다.
We listen to the New Year's bell stroke.

□ 기념일을 축하합니다.
We celebrate our anniversaries.

 Notes

catch up 최신 정보를 알리다   grave 무덤, 묘   pull out 끄집어내다, 뜯어내다   weed 잡초
fly a flag 국기를 달다   set up 세우다, 고정시키다   bell stroke 타종, 종치는 소리

Chapter 10

학교
School

01 대학 지원하기   02 수강 신청 하기   03 강의실에서
04 과제물, 시험 준비   05 성적

01 대학 지원하기

외국 대학을 준비하는 경우 filled-out application form(입학 지원서) 외에도 ecommendation letters(추천서) 등이 필요하죠. tuition(등록금)이 걱정이라면 각 학교의 scholarships (장학금) 제도도 꼭 챙겨 봐야겠습니다.

□ 가고 싶은 대학이 어디야?	What university do you want to go?
	What university do you want to enter?
	Any school you want to go?
□ 학교에 대해 알아봤어?	Have you looked into schools?
	Have you searched any school information?
□ 입학 요강이 인터넷에 공고됐어.	The admission requirements of the school have been posted on the Internet.
	*admission = entrance
□ 입학 설명회는 가 봤어?	Have you attended a university briefing session on its admission requirements?
□ 등록금은 얼마야?	How much is the tuition?
□ 장학금 혜택은 있어?	Are there any scholarships available?
□ 어떤 공부를 하고 싶니?	What do you want to study?
	What major will you be studying?
□ 실용 학문을 하고 싶어.	I want to study something practical.
□ 요즘 취업이 힘드니까.	The job market is quite tough these days.

☐ 입학에 필요한 서류가 뭐야?	What documents do I need for an admission?
	What documents are required for an admission?
☐ 입학 요강은 학교마다 달라.	Each school has different admission requirements.
☐ 대학 홈페이지에서 알아보려고.	I'm going to check out the school homepage.
☐ 언제까지 접수해야 해?	When is the deadline for the application?
	When is the last day for the application?
☐ 서류 작성 요령은 알아?	Do you know how to fill out the application form?
☐ 영문 에세이도 써야 해?	Do I need to write an essay in English, too?
☐ 준비할 것이 정말 많구나.	There are tons of things to prepare for the application.
	A lot of preparations are needed for the application.
☐ 합격했어.	I've been accepted.
	They let me in.
	I've made it.
☐ 방금 합격 통지서 받았어.	I just received the acceptance letter from the school.
☐ 전액 장학금 받았어.	I've got a four-year, full(-ride) scholarship.
☐ 부분 장학금 받았어.	I've got a partial scholarship.

02 수강 신청 하기

MP3를 들어보세요 10-U02

class schedule(강의 시간표)을 짤 때 이번 semester(학기)에 몇 학점을 들 것인지, 어떤 과목을 선택할 것인지를 결정하는 것은 아주 중요합니다. 과목별 성격에 따라 required course(필수 과목), elective course(교양 과목) 등으로 나뉘지요.

원어민 발음 듣기 ☑☐   회화 훈련 ☐☐   듣기 훈련 ☐☐

☐ 이번 학기 몇 학점 들을 거야?
How many credits will you be taking?

☐ 이번 학기 어떤 과목 들을 거야?
What courses will you be taking?

☐ 필수 과목이야.
It's a required course.
*require=mandatory, compulsory

☐ 선택 과목이야.
It's an elective course.
*elective=optional

☐ 그 과목은 예비 과목이 있어.
It has preliminary courses.

☐ 강의 시간표 다 짰어?
Did you make out your class schedule?
*make out=lay out

☐ 수강 신청 마감이 언제야?
When is the deadline for signing up for the classes?

When is the deadline for the class registration?

☐ 이번 주까지야.
The deadline is this week.

You have to register this week.

☐ 신청 과목을 변경하고 싶은데요.
I'd like to change my courses.
*change=switch

Is it okay to change my courses now?

강의실에서

강의실에서는 먼저 학생들의 attendance check(출석 체크)를 하고 수업을 시작하죠. 학기 초에는 the course schedule(강의 계획표)를 나눠 주기도 하고요. 그 밖에 교수님이 강의를 하면서 쓰는 표현, 수업을 듣고 난 후 학생들의 평가 등의 표현을 살펴보겠습니다.

원어민 발음 듣기 ☑☐   회화 훈련 ☐☐   듣기 훈련 ☐☐

□ 출석 체크하겠습니다.
Let me check attendance.
Attendance check!

□ 여기요!
(I'm) Here!
Yes!
Present!

□ 강의 시작합시다.
Let's get started.
Shall we begin?

□ 책 24페이지를 펴세요.
Turn to page 24.
Open your book to page 24.

□ 페이지 넘겨 주세요.
Turn the page, please.
Turn to the next page.

□ 저번 시간에 어디까지 했죠?
Where were we last time?
Does anyone know where we stopped last time?

□ 이것에 대해 아는 사람?
Who knows about this?
Anyone who has a thought about this?

□ 알겠어요? / 이해했어요?
Do you understand me?
Everyone understand?

□ 오늘은 여기까지.	That's all for today. We have to stop here. It's time to finish.
□ 나머지는 다음 시간에 끝낼게요.	We'll finish the rest of this chapter next time. We'll do the rest of it next time.
□ 다음 시간은 이것에 대해 배우겠습니다.	Our next class is about this. We'll talk about this next time.
□ 아직 수업 안 끝났어요.	I'm not done yet. The class is not finished yet.
□ 질문 있어요?	Does anyone have questions? Any questions?
□ 수업이 재미있었어요.	The class was fun. I really enjoyed the class.
□ 시간이 금방 갔어.	Time flew. Time passed quickly.
□ 강의가 훌륭했어요.	The class was great.
□ 수업이 지루했어요.	The class was boring.
□ 그 교수님은 (아주) 열정적이셔.	The professor is very passionate.
□ 그 교수님은 아주 인기가 많으셔.	The professor is immensely popular.
□ 필기를 많이 해야 해.	I have to take notes a lot. *take notes = write down
□ 우리 교수님은 말이 너무 빨라.	Our professor talks too fast.

과제물, 시험 준비

미국에서의 school paper(과제물)와 mid/final term(시험)은 유형이 다양한데, 보통 학생들은 그룹을 지어 주제에 대해 함께 조사하고 공부합니다. 물론 때때로 cramming(벼락치기)을 하는 경우도 있습니다.

수업 끝나고 제출하세요.	Hand in your paper after the class.
이번 주 금요일까지 리포트 제출해요.	You have to hand in the paper by Friday. *hand in = turn in Don't forget to hand in your paper by Friday. The due date for the paper is this Friday.
자세한 내용은 인터넷 게시판 참조.	Please check out the Internet notice for more details.
다음 주엔 총정리 시간을 가질 거예요.	We'll have review hours next week. Next week, we'll review what we've studied so far.
시험은 객관식입니다.	It's a multiple choice test.
시험은 주관식입니다.	It's an essay type test.
2시간 동안 오픈북 테스트입니다.	It will be a two-hour open book test.
부정행위가 적발되면 F학점입니다.	If you cheat, you'll get an F.
시험 잘 보세요.	Good luck for your exam. Good luck to you all.
과제물이 너무 많아요.	We have too many assignments.

□ 그룹 스터디 하자.	Let's study in groups.
	Why don't we make a study group?
□ 중간고사가 언제야?	When is the mid-term?
□ 시험 범위가 어디야?	What should we study?
	The test covers from where to where?
□ 시험공부 하나도 못 했는데.	I haven't studied at all.
□ 벼락치기 해야겠다.	I'm going to cram for the exam.
□ 밤새 벼락치기 했어.	I crammed all night.
□ 시험 어땠어?	How was the exam?
□ (아주) 어려웠어.	It was (unbelievably) hard.
	It was very tough.
□ 어렵지 않았어.	It wasn't so hard.
	It was a piece of cake.
□ (아주) 잘 본 것 같아.	I think I did (pretty) well.
□ 시간이 없었어.	I needed more time.
	I lacked time.
□ 망쳤어.	I screwed up (the exam).
	I messed up (the exam).
	I failed the exam.

 Notes

hand in (서류 등을) 제출하다 assignment 숙제, 과제, 임무 cram 억지로 외우게 하다, 주입하다 unbelievably 믿을 수 없을 만큼, 무척 a piece of cake 무척 하기 쉬운 것(일)

05 성적

GPA는 grade point average를 줄인 말로 우리말로 '평점'이라는 뜻입니다. 이 GPA가 나쁠 경우 retaking(재수강)을 해야 하거나 취업 시 나쁜 영향을 끼칠 수 있으니 잘 관리하는 것이 중요합니다.

원어민 발음 듣기 ☑□   회화 훈련 □□   듣기 훈련 □□

성적이 좋아.	I got good grades. I got a good GPA.
성적이 안 좋아.	I got bad grades. I got a bad GPA.
성적 확인했어?	Did you check your grades? What are your grades? *grade(s) = GPA
성적이 이상해.	Something went wrong with my grades. There must be some mistakes with my grades.
교수님께 여쭤봐야지.	I need to talk to my professor. I'm going to ask him about my grades.
낙제하면 어쩌지?	What if I am flunked? What if I fail the course?
재수강해야겠다.	I'm going to retake the course. I need to repeat the course.
이번 학기에 그녀가 수석이야.	She is the top of the class for this semester.

Chapter 11

직장
Workplace

01 구직 활동   02 면접 보기   03 첫 출근   04 회의 및 보고   05 식사, 휴식시간
06 지각, 결근, 휴가   07 거래처 방문, 손님 접대   08 출장

구직 활동

job hunting(구직) 할 때 여러 job-search websites(구직 사이트)에서 실속 있는 job openings(일자리 정보)를 얻어야겠죠. résumé(이력서), cover letter(자기 소개서), certificate of graduation(졸업 증명서) 등 필요한 서류를 미리 준비해 두는 것이 좋습니다.

원어민 발음 듣기 ☑☐   회화 훈련 ☐☐   듣기 훈련 ☐☐

☐ 일자리를 찾고 있어.
I'm looking for a job.
*job = position

☐ 어떤 일자리를 원해?
What kind of work do you want?
What kind of job are you looking for?

☐ 구직 사이트를 확인해 봤어?
Have you checked the Internet job-search websites?
Did you search for job opportunities on the Internet?

☐ 좋은 일자리 정보를 얻었어.
I've found some great job openings.
*job openings = hiring information

☐ 마땅한 일자리 정보가 없어.
I can't find anything good for me.

☐ 입사 지원에 필요한 서류는 뭐야?
What do you need to prepare for the job appli-cation?
What documents do you need for the job appli-cation?

☐ 입사 지원서, 졸업 증명서, 자기 소개서, 추천서야.
I need a filed-out job application form, a certi-ficate of graduation, a letter of introduction, and reference letters.

☐ 이력서와 자기 소개서가 필요해.
I need a detailed résumé and cover letter.
I need to submit a résumé and letter.

☐ 합격자 발표는 언제야?	When do they announce successful candidates?
	When will they let you know the result?
☐ 합격자에게 따로 전화한대.	They will call each successful candidate separately.
☐ 전화를 기다리고 있어.	I'm waiting for a call from the company.
☐ 전화가 안 와.	I haven't heard from them.
☐ 나 합격했어.	I got the job.
	I've made it.
☐ 다음 주부터 출근해.	I start from next week.
☐ 나 떨어졌어.	I didn't get the job.
☐ 자격 미달이래.	They said I was underqualified.
☐ 나이가 많대.	They said I'm too old for the job.
	They said I went over the age limit.
☐ 다른 회사 알아봐야지.	I'll start looking (for a job) again.

📑 Notes

prepare for ~을 준비하다 certificate 졸업 증명서(=diploma) detailed 자세한, 상세한
submit (서류 등을) 제출하다 announce 공식적으로 발표하다 successful candidate 합격자 separately 따로 start from ~부터 시작하다 underqualified 자격이 안 되는, 자격 미달의 age limit 나이 제한

02 면접 보기

job interview(면접)에서 자주 등장하는 질문과 가능한 대답을 살펴보겠습니다. campus life(대학 생활)와 major(전공), 자신의 strengths(강점)와 weaknesses(약점), career(경력) 등을 말하는 다양한 표현도 같이 알아둡시다.

원어민 발음 듣기 ☑□ 회화 훈련 □□ 듣기 훈련 □□

면접이 언제야?	When is your job interview?
단정한 옷차림을 해.	Dress neat and tidy.
면접에 늦지 마.	Don't be late for the interview. Be there on time.
면접 전에 리허설을 해 봐.	Why don't you have a rehearsal before the interview? Rehearse before the actual interview.
자신에 대해 소개해 보세요.	Why don't you introduce yourself to us? Tell us about yourself.
저는 경제학을 전공했습니다.	I studied economics in college.
당신의 강점과 약점은 무엇입니까?	What are your strengths and weaknesses? Tell us about your strengths and weaknesses.
활발하고 성실하며 끈기가 있습니다.	I'm very active, sincere, and patient.
저는 일중독 성향이 있습니다.	I could be a workaholic.
대학 생활은 어땠나요?	How was your school life? *school life = campus life

많은 친구들을 사귀었습니다.	I've made lots of friends.
왜 이 회사를 선택했나요?	Why did you choose our company? Is there any reason why you picked our company?
제가 꿈에 그리던 직장입니다.	It's my dream job. I always wanted to work for the company like this.
이전 직장에 대해 말해 보세요.	Let us know about your previous work. Tell us about your previous work.
마케팅 회사에서 3년간 일했습니다.	I worked for the marketing company for three years.
왜 그만두었나요?	Why did you quit? Why did you leave your previous work?
자신의 경력에 대해 말해 보세요.	Would you please tell me about your career?
수출입 업무에 경험이 많습니다.	I have a lot of experience in importing and exporting.
본인이 창의적인 사람이라고 생각해요?	Do you consider yourself a creative person? Do you think you're creative?
면접 어땠어?	How was the interview? How did the interview go?
너무 떨렸어.	I was extremely nervous.
침착해지려고 애썼어.	I tried to be calm. *calm = cool

03 첫 출근

first day at work(첫 출근 날)에는 함께 일할 직원들을 소개 받고 간단히 사무실 투어를 합니다. staff training(직원 교육)을 통해 회사 규칙 등을 배우고 자리도 배정 받죠. probie(수습사원)로서 회의에 참석하거나 다양한 경험들을 하게 됩니다.

원어민 발음 듣기 ☑□   회화 훈련 □□   듣기 훈련 □□

□ 입사를 환영합니다.	Welcome aboard!
	Nice to have you with us.
□ 입사 첫날 어때요?	How is your first day going (so far)?
□ 모든 것이 너무 빨라요.	Everything's moving very fast.
□ 곧 익숙해져요.	You'll get used to it.
□ 잘 보고 배우세요.	Watch and learn.
□ 선배를 잘 따라 하세요.	Just follow what your seniors do.
□ 그는 당신보다 1년 먼저 입사했어요.	He joined this company one year before you.
	*join = enter
□ 우리는 입사 동기예요.	We joined the company the same year.
□ 수습 기간은 3개월입니다.	Your probation will be for three months.
	You will be a probie for three months.
□ 어려운 점은 상사와 의논하세요.	If you have difficulties, talk to your boss.
□ 어려울 땐 저에게 오세요.	If you feel difficult, come to me.

☐ 신입 사원을 소개합니다.	Let me introduce our new employees.
	Here are our new members of the staff.
☐ 잘 부탁합니다.	I depend on all of you.
☐ 뭐든지 시켜 주세요.	I'm at your service.
☐ 자리가 여기예요.	This is your desk. *desk = cubicle
☐ 간단히 사무실 투어를 하겠습니다.	Let me give you a quick office tour.
☐ 직원들을 소개시켜 드릴게요.	Allow me to introduce you to people you'll be working with.
☐ 업무 시작합시다.	Let's get started.
	Let's get to work.
☐ 오늘 주간 회의 있습니다.	We have a weekly staff meeting today.
☐ 모두 회의에 참석하세요.	All staff members make sure to attend the meeting.
☐ 오늘이 마감 날입니다.	Today is the deadline.
	We have the deadline today.

📝 Notes

aboard 새로운 멤버로서, 신입자로서   move fast 빠르게 움직이다(돌아가다)   get used to ~에 익숙해지다   join the company 회사에 입사하다(= enter the company)   probation 수습(견습) 기간   probie 견습생, 수습 사원   cubicle 칸막이가 처진 좁은 장소   office tour 사무실 둘러보기   staff meeting 직원 회의   make sure 확실히 해 두다

04 회의 및 보고

MP3를 들어보세요 11-U04

conference(회의)에서는 주요 issues(안건)에 대한 의견을 나누고 찬성과 반대를 결정합니다. 업무 진행 과정에 대한 간단한 briefing(브리핑)이나 상세한 presentation(프레젠테이션)이 이뤄지기도 하죠. 복잡하고 어려운 문제에 대해서는 이를 철저히 분석하고 맡아서 처리할 사람을 결정하기도 합니다.

원어민 발음 듣기 ☑□   회화 훈련 □□   듣기 훈련 □□

□ 회의합시다.
Let's have a meeting.
Let's start a meeting.

□ 회의 주제가 뭡니까?
What are the issues for the meeting?
What are you covering on the meeting?

□ 논의할 세 가지 안건이 있습니다.
We have three issues to discuss.
*issues = items, topics, matters, agendas

□ 첫 번째 안건은 이것입니다.
First is this.

□ 다음 안건은 이것입니다.
The next matter is this.

□ 마지막 안건은 이것입니다.
And the last one is this.

□ 다음 안건입니다.
Move on to the next topic.
Can we go on to the next item?
Next agenda, please.

□ 만장일치입니다.
It's a unanimous decision.
We've unanimously agreed on this.

□ 반대하는 사람 있나요?
Is there anyone who doesn't agree?
Anyone who opposes this?

☐ 이 건에 대해선 다시 회의합시다.	Let's talk more about this later.
	Let's have another meeting later.
☐ 브리핑하세요.	Give us a briefing.
☐ 프레젠테이션을 시작하겠습니다.	I'll start my presentation.
	Let me start my presentation.
☐ 건의사항 있습니까?	Do you have any suggestions?
	*suggestions = recommendations
☐ 문제점이 무엇입니까?	What seems to be the problem?
	What are the problems?
☐ 해결책이 있나요?	Do we have any answers?
	*answers = solutions
☐ 이 문제를 처리할 사람?	Does anyone want to handle this problem?
	Does anyone want to take care of this?
☐ 제가 해 보겠습니다.	I'll do it.
	I'll give it a shot.
	I think I can take care of it.
☐ 변동 사항은 즉시 보고하세요.	If there are any changes, report to me right away.
	*right away = immediately

Notes

unanimous 만장일치의 brief 요점을 간략하게 보고하다 take care of ~을 처리(해결)하다 give it a shot 한번 시도해 보다 let ~ know ~에게 알려 주다

05 식사, 휴식 시간

바쁜 오전 업무가 끝나고 점심시간이 되면 항상 "무엇을 먹을까?", "어디서 먹을까?" 고민합니다. 보통 cafeteria(구내식당)을 이용하지만 회사 밖에 있는 restaurants(음식점)에 가는 경우도 있습니다. 식사 후에는 coffee break(커피를 마시며 휴식하는 시간)을 가지기도 합니다.

원어민 발음 듣기 ☑☐   회화 훈련 ☐☐   듣기 훈련 ☐☐

☐ 오늘 점심 뭘 먹을까요?	What should we eat for lunch? *eat = have
☐ 어디에서 먹을까요?	Where should we eat?
☐ 구내식당 갈까요?	Shall we eat in the cafeteria?
☐ 나가서 먹어요.	Let's eat outside. Why don't we go out for lunch?
☐ 점심 약속이 있어요.	I already have a lunch plan. I'm going to have lunch with someone.
☐ 쉬었다 합시다.	Let's take a break. Let's take 5.
☐ 커피 한잔 합시다.	Take a coffee break? How about some coffee?
☐ 식곤증 나요.	I feel drowsy after lunch.
☐ 잠시 외출할게요.	I'll be out for a minute.
☐ 누가 찾으면 문자 주세요.	If anyone wants me, please text me.
☐ 쉴 틈도 없어.	We don't have time for a break.
☐ 다시 일합시다.	Let's get back to work.

06 지각, 결근, 휴가

being late for work(지각)나 day-off(결근)를 할 때, 혹은 taking vacation(휴가 신청) 할 때에는 회사에 합당한 이유를 밝혀야 합니다. 무단으로 회사를 나오지 않을 경우 심각한 문제에 직면할 수도 있습니다. 몸이 아프거나 출산을 앞둔 경우라면 sick leave(병가)나 maternity leave(출산 휴가)를 냅니다.

원어민 발음 듣기 ☑□   회화 훈련 □□   듣기 훈련 □□

늦어서 죄송합니다.	I'm sorry I'm late.
그는 또 지각이야.	He's late again.
그는 항상 늦게 출근해.	He's always late for work.
다시는 이런 일이 없도록 하겠습니다.	It won't happen again.
	I promise it will never happen again.
내일 조금 늦게 출근하겠습니다.	I'll be coming in a little late tomorrow.
	Can I come in a little late tomorrow?
이유가 뭡니까?	What's the reason?
	Tell me why.
내일 아침에 건강 검진이 있어요.	I have a physical exam tomorrow morning.
저 오늘 조퇴하겠습니다.	Can I take the rest of the day off?
	May I leave early today?
몸이 안 좋아요.	My condition is not so good.
	I don't feel good today.
집에 급한 일이 생겼어요.	I have an urgent matter at home.
삼촌이 돌아가셨어요.	My uncle passed away.

☐ 집에 가세요.	You can go. *go = leave
☐ 오늘 출근 못하겠습니다.	I don't think I can make it today.
☐ 그는 오늘 무단결근했어.	He took a day off without notice. He didn't come in without calling.
☐ 월차를 내고 싶습니다.	I'd like to take a day off.
☐ 내일 병가를 내겠습니다.	I'd like to get sick leave tomorrow.
☐ 여름휴가 일정을 잡고 싶어요.	I'd like to schedule my summer vacation.
☐ 출산 휴가를 내겠습니다.	I'm going to take maternity leave.
☐ 내일부터 휴가야.	My vacation starts from tomorrow.
☐ 휴가 때 어디 가?	Are you going somewhere during your holidays?
☐ 해외여행 가려고.	I'm planning an overseas trip. I'm preparing for a trip abroad.
☐ 집에서 푹 쉬려고.	I'm going to relax at home.
☐ 잠이나 실컷 자려고.	I'm going to oversleep.
☐ 바닷가에 가려고.	I'm going to the beach.
☐ 휴가 때 전화하지 마.	Don't call me while I'm on my vacation.
☐ 휴대폰 꺼 놓을 거야.	My cell phone will be off.

📖 Notes

come in 회사에 출근하다   physical exam 건강 검진(= general check-up)   rest of the day 남은 하루   urgent 긴급한, 응급의   pass away 죽다, 돌아가시다   make it 해내다, 성공하다   take a day off 월차를 내다(쓰다), 하루 쉬다   maternity leave 출산 휴가   overseas trip 해외여행(= trip abroad)

07 거래처 방문, 손님 접대

working outside(외근)의 종류는 다양하지만 흔히 거래처를 방문하는 일이 많습니다. 손님으로서 다른 회사를 찾아가는 경우와 반대로 외부 손님을 자신이 근무하는 회사에서 접대하는 경우에 쓸 수 있는 표현을 알아보겠습니다.

□ 오늘 외근합니다.	I'll work outside today.
	I'll be out today.
□ 거래처에서 부르네요.	Our client wants to see me.
□ 다른 업무도 처리하고 올게요.	I'll take care of other things, too.
□ 외근 뒤 바로 퇴근하겠습니다.	After that, I'll go straight home.
	After that, I'll go home without coming in.
□ 손님이 오셨어요.	We have clients here.
□ 접견실로 모셔 주세요.	Why don't you guide them to the reception room?
□ 마실 것을 대접해 주세요.	Would you serve drinks to them?
□ 이쪽입니다.	This way, please.
□ 중요한 손님입니다.	They're very important clients.
□ 정중히 대접하세요.	Take extra good care of them.

 Notes

straightly 바로, 곧바로 guide 안내하다, 인도하다 serve 대접하다

출장

회사 생활에서 국내 또는 해외로의 business trip(출장)이 불가피할 때가 있습니다. 특히 해외 출장의 경우 빡빡한 출장 일정뿐만 아니라 장거리인 경우 jet lag(시차증)로 고생하기도 하죠.

저 출장 갑니다.	I'm going for a business trip.
며칠 사무실을 비웁니다.	I'll be away from the office for a few days.
	I'm out of town for a couple of days.
며칠간 출장이십니까?	How long will you be gone?
이틀이요.	I'll be on a business trip for two days.
출장 일정이 아주 빡빡해요.	The schedule is very tight.
누구와 동행하십니까?	Who will you go with?
혼자 갑니다.	I'll go alone.
상사를 모시고 갑니다.	I'll go with my boss.
잘 다녀오셨어요?	Welcome back!
출장 어땠어요?	How was your business trip?
아주 바빴어요.	I was crazily busy.
한숨도 못 잤어요.	I couldn't sleep at all.
시차증이 있어요.	I have the jet lag.
	I'm jet-lagged.

Chapter 12

음식
Food

01 좋아하는 음식 **02** 식사 주문하기 **03** 술자리에서 **04** 식당 평가 **05** 계산하기

좋아하는 음식

서로 다른 취향, 특히 좋아하는 음식에 대해 이야기하다 보면 처음 만난 사이라도 어색함이 금방 사라집니다. 어떤 종류의 음식을 좋아하는지, 요리를 할 줄 아는지, 잘하는 요리가 있는지 등을 어떻게 물어보는지 알아봅시다.

원어민 발음 듣기 ☑☐   회화 훈련 ☐☐   듣기 훈련 ☐☐

□ 어떤 음식 좋아해?	What kind of food do you like? *food = dish, meal
□ 가장 좋아하는 음식은 뭐니?	What's your favorite food? What do you like the most?
□ 한식은 다 좋아해.	I like all Korean foods.
□ 난 이탈리아 음식이 좋아.	I love Italian foods.
□ 특별한 날엔 어떤 음식을 먹어?	What do you eat on a special day?
□ 요리 잘해?	Are you a good cook? Do you cook well?
□ 가장 잘하는 요리는 뭐야?	What's your specialty?
□ 레시피 좀 가르쳐 줘.	Can I have the recipe? Do you mind if you give me the recipe?
□ 간식을 좋아하니?	Do you like snacks?
□ 난 과일을 즐겨 먹어.	I enjoy eating fruits.
□ 주로 어떤 차를 마시니?	What do you usually drink?
□ 커피와 녹차를 주로 마셔.	I drink coffee and green tea.

식사 주문하기

식당에서 음식을 주문할 때는 I'll have ~. 또는 I'm going to have ~.(~을 먹을게요.)라고 합니다. 식사 중간에 필요한 것을 요청할 때, 취향에 따라 직접 골라야 하는 경우, 테이블 정리를 부탁할 때 어떻게 말하는지 살펴봅시다.

원어민 발음 듣기 ☑□   회화 훈련 □□   듣기 훈련 □□

□ 어서 오세요.
Welcome.
Come right in.

□ 일행이 몇 분이세요?
How many are with you?
How many (are) in your party?

□ 네 명 자리 주세요.
We need a table for four.
A table for four, please.

□ 창가 자리로 주시겠어요?
I'd like a table by the window.
A window table, please.

□ 조용한 자리로 주시겠어요?
I'd like quiet seats.
Quiet seats, please.

□ 메뉴판 주세요.
Can I see the menu?
Can we have the menu?
The menu, please.

□ 나눠서 먹자.
Let's share the food.
Shall we share the food?

□ 주문할게요.
We're ready to order.
We're going to order.

□ 주문하시겠어요?
Would you like to order?
May I take your order?

	Are you ready to order?
☐ 한 사람이 더 올 거예요.	I'm expecting someone.
☐ 잠시 후에 주문할게요.	We'll order a little later.
☐ 여기는 어떤 음식을 잘 하나요?	What's your specialty? What's good here?
☐ 새로운 것을 먹어 볼래.	I'll try something new.
☐ 아직 결정 못했어요.	We haven't decided yet.
☐ 결정되면 부를게요.	We'll call you when we're ready.
☐ 스테이크로 먹을게요.	I'll have steak. I'll try steak. I'm going to have steak.
☐ 우리가 주문한 것이 아닌데요.	This isn't what we ordered.
☐ 음식이 아직 안 나왔어요.	I haven't got my food yet.
☐ 식탁 좀 치워 주세요.	Could you please clear the table?
☐ 물 좀 더 주세요.	Can I get some more water? I want some more water.
☐ 반찬 좀 더 주세요.	I'd like to have more of this side dish.
☐ 후식은 무엇으로 하시겠어요?	What would you like for dessert? Would you like dessert?
☐ 커피 주세요.	(Just) Coffee, please.
☐ 남은 음식은 싸 주시겠어요?	Could you please wrap this up? Can I have a doggie bag?

03 술자리에서

MP3를 들어보세요 12-U03

식사 자리에서 술을 권할 때는 Want a drink?라고 하면 됩니다. 술을 한잔 사겠다고 할 때는 I'll buy you a drink.라고 하고, 주량을 물어볼 때는 How much do you drink?라고 하죠. 이 밖에도 건배 제의하기, 취했을 때 등의 표현들을 배워 보겠습니다.

원어민 발음 듣기 ☑☐ 회화 훈련 ☐☐ 듣기 훈련 ☐☐

☐ 술 한잔 하고 싶다.	I'd like to have a drink.
	I feel like drinking.
☐ 술 한잔 할래?	Would you like to have a drink?
	Want a drink?
	How about a drink?
☐ 내가 한잔 살게.	I'll buy you a drink.
☐ 술을 주문할까?	Let's order some alcohol.
☐ 맥주 주세요.	Can I have a beer?
☐ 와인 한 병 주세요.	Can I have a bottle of wine?
☐ 어떤 와인으로 드릴까요?	What kind of wine would you like?
☐ 가장 인기 있는 것으로 주세요.	The most popular wine here, please.
☐ 건배!	Let's toast. / Cheers! / Chin-chin!
☐ 모두들, 원샷!	Everybody, bottoms up!
☐ 건강을 위하여!	To our health!
☐ 술 좋아해?	Do you like drinking?
	Do you enjoy drinking?
☐ 주량이 보통 얼마야?	How much do you usually drink?
	What's your limit?

175

☐ 난 술이 세.	I drink like a fish.
	I'm a heavy drinker.
☐ 난 술이 약해.	I'm a lightweight.
☐ 전혀 못 마셔.	I don't drink.
	Not even a drop.
☐ 난 사람이 좋아서 술을 마셔.	I'm a social drinker.
	I love drinking with people.
☐ 술을 천천히 마시는 편이야.	I'm a slow drinker.
☐ 가능하면 안 마시려고 해.	I try not to drink.
☐ 술 마시는 거 좋아하지 않아.	I don't like drinking.
☐ 나 술 끊었어.	I quit drinking.
☐ 일주일에 두 번 마셔.	I drink twice a week.
☐ 나 취하는 것 같은데.	I think I'm getting drunk.
☐ 나 안 취했어.	I'm not drunk.
☐ 이제 그만 마셔야겠다.	I think I should stop here.
	That's it for me.
☐ 토할 것 같아.	I don't feel good.
	I think I'm going to throw up.
☐ 머리가 핑핑 돌아.	I feel dizzy.
	My head is spinning.
☐ 그는 엄청 취했어.	He's totally wasted.
☐ 그는 주사가 심해.	He's out of control when he gets drunk.
☐ 어젯밤에 나 필름 끊겼어.	I blacked out last night.
	*black out = pass out

04 식당 평가

식당에 가면 그 집의 taste(맛)와 service(서비스)를 평가하게 됩니다. 아무리 famous restaurant (맛집)이라도 그 reputation(명성)과 달리 실망스러운 경우도 있지요. 음식의 맛과 서비스에 대한 표현은 어떤 것이 있는지 살펴보겠습니다.

원어민 발음 듣기 ☑□   회화 훈련 □□   듣기 훈련 □□

□ 음식이 맛있다.	The food is delicious.
	It tastes wonderful.
	*wonderful = tasty, superb, fabulous
□ 처음 먹어 보는 맛이야.	I've never tasted like this before.
□ 역시 소문대로야.	It has lived up to its reputation.
□ 음식이 형편없어.	The food is horrible.
	*horrible = awful
□ 유명한 집 맞아?	Is this really a famous restaurant?
□ 서비스가 최고야.	The service here is great.
□ 서비스가 엉망이야.	The service here is really bad.
□ 너무 불친절해.	They are very rude.
□ 너무 비싸다.	It's too expensive.
□ 거기 다시는 안 갈 거야.	I'll never go there again.
□ 매니저 불러 주세요.	Call your manager, please.
	I'd like to have a word with your manager.

 Notes

horrible 끔찍하게 나쁜, 오싹한   post 붙이다, 게시하다   have a word with ~와 잠깐 이야기하다, ~에게 잔소리하다

05 계산하기

미국에서는 같이 먹은 음식 값을 계산할 때 보통 go Dutch(각자 내다)하지만 특별한 경우 I'll get this. 혹은 I got it.(내가 살게.)이라고 말하는 때도 있습니다. 반반씩 부담할 경우에는 간단히 Go 50-50.라고 하면 됩니다.

원어민 발음 듣기 ☑☐   회화 훈련 ☐☐   듣기 훈련 ☐☐

☐ 계산서 주세요.	Check, please. *check = bill Can we have the bill?
☐ 내가 살게.	It's on me. My treat. I'll get this (one). I got it.
☐ 아냐, 내가 살게.	No, let me. Please, allow me.
☐ 다음에 사 줘.	Why don't you buy me next time?
☐ 디저트는 네가 사.	Why don't you buy me dessert?
☐ 각자 내자.	Let's go Dutch. Let's pay separately. Let's split it.
☐ 반씩 내자.	Let's go fifty-fifty. *fifty-fifty = halves
☐ 어디서 계산하죠?	Where can I pay?
☐ 계산이 이상해요.	I think there's a mistake on the bill.
☐ 다시 확인해 주세요.	Would you please check again?

Chapter 13

쇼핑
Shopping

01 매장에서   02 상품 비교, 선택하기   03 가격 흥정하기
04 계산, 포장하기   05 교환, 환불하기

매장에서

매장을 찾거나 매장 내에서 원하는 물건을 찾을 때 I'm looking for ~. (~를 찾고 있어요.)라고 말합니다. store clerk(점원)은 new arrivals(신상품)와 sale items(세일 상품)가 진열된 곳으로 안내해 주기도 하고 일시 품절된 상품을 order in advance(선주문)해 주기도 합니다.

원어민 발음 듣기 ☑□ 회화 훈련 □□ 듣기 훈련 □□

□ 여성 옷은 몇 층에 있나요?	Which floor is women's clothing?
	Where can I find women's wear?
	*wear = apparel
□ 5층으로 가세요.	It's on the fifth floor.
□ 중앙 에스컬레이터를 이용하세요.	Use the escalator in the middle.
□ '샤넬' 매장을 찾는데요.	I'm looking for Chanel.
□ 그 매장은 없어졌어요.	That shop is no longer here.
□ 특별히 찾으시는 상품이 있나요?	Are you looking for something in particular?
□ 도와드릴까요?	Can I help you?
	Can I help you find something?
□ 카디건을 찾는데요.	I'm looking for a cardigan.
□ 신상품은 이쪽입니다.	New arrival items are displayed here.
	You can check out new items here.
□ 이 신발 245mm 있나요?	Do you have these shoes in size 245?
	*사이즈 245mm = 7 ½
□ 창고에 가서 확인해 보겠습니다.	I'll check in our stock room.
	Let me check our storage room.

☐ 그 상품은 일시 품절입니다.	The item is not available right now. *item = product
☐ 다 팔렸습니다.	We're sold-out.
☐ 재고가 없습니다.	We're out of stock. We're out of it at the moment.
☐ 일주일 후면 재입고 됩니다.	The item will be restocked in a week. The item will be available in a week.
☐ 선 주문하시겠어요?	Would you like to order in advance?
☐ 도착하면 배송해 드리겠습니다.	When it arrives, we'll deliver the item to your house.
☐ 그런 상품은 없는데요.	We don't have that item. *have = sell, carry
☐ 여기 매장에서 본 적 있어요.	I've seen the item in your store.
☐ 이것도 세일인가요?	Is this a sale item, too?
☐ 그것은 세일 제외 상품입니다.	That is excluded from the sale.

📑 Notes

clothing 의복, 의류   storage 저장, 창고   sold-out 매진된, 품절의   out of stock 재고가 바닥난, 매진되어, 품절되어   restock 새로 보충하다, 다시 들이다   in advance 미리, 사전에, 앞서서   exclude 제외시키다, 빼다

02 상품 비교, 선택하기

구매 전 상품을 비교해 볼 때 쓸 수 있는 표현들을 알아봅시다. 옷 고를 때는 I like the design.(디자인이 마음에 들어요.), You have quite a variety.(제품이 다양하네요.), Can I see the item over there?(저쪽에 있는 상품 보여주세요.) 등의 말을 할 수 있겠죠. 너무 비싸서 다시 생각해 보고 싶으면 I'll think about it. 하고 말하면 됩니다.

원어민 발음 듣기 ☑□　회화 훈련 □□　듣기 훈련 □□

□ 이 옷 디자인이 마음에 들어요.	I like the design of this cloth. *like 대신 love를 쓰면 '매우 좋다'는 의미가 된다.
□ 다른 색깔은 없나요?	Do you have other colors?
□ 검정색과 회색, 두 가지뿐입니다.	We have only black and grey.
□ 두 색 다 잘 어울리시네요.	You look great in black and grey.
□ 입어 보세요.	Why don't you try it on?
□ 탈의실이 어디예요?	Where is the fitting room? *fitting room = changing room
□ 밝은 색이 있으면 좋을 텐데요.	I wish you had brighter colors.
□ 이 상품은 어떠세요?	How would you like this one?
□ 그 디자인은 별로예요.	I don't like the design.
□ 저쪽에 있는 상품을 보여 주세요.	Let me see the product over there. Can I see the item over there?
□ 마네킹이 입은 옷을 입어 보고 싶어요.	I'd like to try on the clothes that a mannequin is wearing.
□ 둘 다 주세요.	I'll take (them) both.
□ 재킷이 약간 작네요.	This jacket is a little small (for me).
□ 이 옷은 너무 꽉 껴요.	This is too tight.

☐ 이 옷은 너무 커요.	This is too loose.
☐ 사이즈가 딱 맞네요.	It's a perfect fit for you. It fits you perfectly. It's just right for you.
☐ 요즘 유행이에요.	This is in style now. This is the trend at the moment. It's the most popular these days.
☐ 날씬해 보이세요.	You look thin in those clothes.
☐ 한 치수 작은 것으로 할게요.	I'd like to have this in a smaller size. Can I have a smaller one?
☐ 좀 더 생각해 볼게요.	I'll think about it. I need more time to think.
☐ 좀 더 둘러볼게요.	I want to look around more.
☐ 다시 들를게요.	I'll come back later.

03 가격 흥정하기

MP3를 들어보세요 13-U03

가격 흥정을 할 때는 주로 Can you give me a discount?(깎아 주시면 안 돼요?)라고 말합니다. 물건을 살 때 현금으로 지불하면 할인을 받을 수 있는지, 여러 개를 구입하면 싸게 살 수 있는지 등 가격을 흥정할 때 쓰는 여러 가지 표현을 알아보겠습니다.

원어민 발음 듣기 ☑☐   회화 훈련 ☐☐   듣기 훈련 ☐☐

☐ 가격이 얼마예요?	How much (is this)? How much does it cost?
☐ 가격표가 없네요.	I can't find the price tag on this.
☐ 너무 비싼 것 같아요.	I think it's too expensive. It's way out of my price range. It's over my limit.
☐ 깎아 주시면 안 돼요?	Can you give me a discount? Can you give me a better price?
☐ 얼마나 할인해 주실 건데요?	How much discount can you give me?
☐ 두 개 사면 싸게 주시나요?	If I take two, can I get a discount? *take = buy
☐ 현금으로 지불하면 할인되나요?	If I pay in cash, can I get a discount?
☐ 정찰가 판매입니다.	It's a fixed price.
☐ 밑지고 파는 겁니다.	We're making no profit out of it. We're selling them below cost. *cost = price
☐ 싸게 사시는 거예요.	It's a good deal.

04 계산, 포장하기

카드 결제 시에는 pay in a single payment(일시불)로 할 것인지 아니면 pay in installments(할부)로 할 것인지를 물어봅니다. no interest(무이자) 기간을 확인하여 결제하는 것이 현명한 구매 방법이겠죠. 환경을 위해 plastic bag(비닐)이나 paper bag(종이 가방) 대신 가져온 장바구니를 사용하는 것이 좋겠습니다.

원어민 발음 듣기 ☑☐   회화 훈련 ☐☐   듣기 훈련 ☐☐

☐ 계산해 주세요.	I'd like to pay for this.
☐ 어떻게 계산하시겠어요?	How would you like to pay?
☐ 현금, 아니면 카드로 하시겠습니까?	Cash or (credit) card? Cash or charge?
☐ 현금 드릴게요.	I'll pay in cash. Cash.
☐ 카드로 할게요.	I'll pay by credit card. Card. Charge. Do you take credit cards?
☐ 일시불로 계산할게요.	I'd like to pay in a single payment. I'll pay all at once.
☐ 할부로 계산할게요.	I'll pay in installments.
☐ 3개월 무이자 할부로 해 주세요.	No interest for three months, please.
☐ 종이백이나 비닐봉지 필요하세요?	Do you need a paper or plastic bag?
☐ 선물용 포장해 주세요.	Can I get this gift-wrapped? Could you gift-wrap it? Giftwrap, please.

05 교환, 환불하기

구입한 상품을 exchanges(교환), refunds(환불)할 때는 보통 구입 후 일정 기간 내에 상품의 하자가 없는 상태에서 상품과 영수증을 가져가면 됩니다. 교환의 경우 difference(차액)가 발생할 수 있습니다.

원어민 발음 듣기 ☑☐ 회화 훈련 ☐☐ 듣기 훈련 ☐☐

☐ 구입 후 일주일 안에 환불, 교환됩니다.	Purchased items can be refunded or exchanged within a week after the purchase of the item.
☐ 물건을 교환하고 싶어요.	I'd like to exchange this.
☐ 물건에 하자가 있어요.	The item is damaged. It has defects.
☐ 제가 그런 게 아니에요.	I didn't do this.
☐ 영수증은 가져오셨어요?	Do you have the receipt (on you)?
☐ 물건을 확인할게요.	Let me check the item.
☐ 어떤 것으로 교환하고 싶으세요?	What would you like to exchange?
☐ 차액은 환불해 주세요.	I'd like to get the rest in cash, please.
☐ (초과된) 차액을 지불할게요.	I'll pay the difference.
☐ 이 물건을 환불하고 싶어요.	I'd like to refund this.
☐ 카드 결제가 취소되었습니다.	The transactions have been cancelled.
☐ 착용한 옷은 교환이나 환불이 안 됩니다.	The clothes you've already worn can't be exchanged or refunded.

Chapter 14

교통
Transportation

01 교통수단 02 교통 상황 03 지하철과 버스 타기 04 택시 타기
05 대중교통 티켓 요금 06 면허 따기, 운전하기 07 주유, 세차하기 08 교통 법규

교통수단

public transportation(대중교통)은 도시 생활을 원활하게 만드는 핵심 수단입니다. 교통 체증 없이 달리는 subway(지하철), 군데군데 닿지 않는 곳이 없는 town bus/city bus(버스), 장거리 여행 시 발이 되어 주는 express bus(고속버스) 등 다양한 교통수단이 있습니다.

원어민 발음 듣기 ☑☐　회화 훈련 ☐☐　듣기 훈련 ☐☐

☐ 출근 시에는 지하철을 타.   I go to work by subway.

☐ 지하철이 사람들로 꽉 찼어.   The subway is packed with people.

☐ 바쁠 때는 택시를 타.   When I'm in a hurry, I take a cab.
*cab=taxi

☐ 어떻게 출퇴근(통학)해?   How do you commute?

☐ 한 번에 가는 버스가 있어.   There's a bus to get there without change.
*change=transfer

☐ 출장 갈 때는 KTX를 타.   I take KTX when I travel on (company) business.

☐ 난 내 차를 운전해.   I drive my own car.

☐ 난 내 차 없이 아무 데도 안 가.   I don't go anywhere without my car.

☐ 하루에 두 번 운행하는 배가 있어.   There's the ferry that runs twice a day.

☐ 일본까지 배 타고 가 본 적 있어?   Have you traveled to Japan by ship?

☐ 여기서부터는 대중교통이 없어.   There's no public transportation from here.

☐ 택시를 부르자.   Let's call a cab.

02 교통 상황

월요일 아침 rush hour(출퇴근 시간)이면 traffic jam(교통 체증)이 유난히 더 심합니다. 라디오에서는 연신 Cars are moving slowly.(차들이 서행합니다.), There's been an accident.(사고가 났습니다.), Please take other roads.(우회하세요.) 등과 같은 보도를 하죠.

원어민 발음 듣기 ☑☐   회화 훈련 ☐☐   듣기 훈련 ☐☐

☐ 지금 교통 상황이 어때?	How are the traffic conditions? How's the road?
☐ 지금 도로가 많이 붐빌 거야.	The road must be busy now. There must be a huge traffic jam. *jam = congestion There must be bumper-to-bumper.
☐ 출퇴근 시간이잖아.	It's the rush hour. It's the morning rush.
☐ 차들이 서행하고 있습니다.	Cars are moving slowly.
☐ 오늘 교통 체증이 매우 심합니다.	The traffic is heavily congested today.
☐ 교통 체증이 유난히 심합니다.	The traffic is heavier than usual.
☐ 다른 길로 우회하세요.	Please detour. Please take other roads.
☐ (대형) 교통사고가 났습니다.	There has been an (major) accident.
☐ 길이 매우 미끄럽습니다.	The roads are very slippery.
☐ 길이 얼었습니다.	The roads are very icy.
☐ 도로가 한가하다.	The traffic is light.

03 지하철과 버스 타기

신촌에서 동대문 시장까지 찾아가는 상황을 가정하여 getting on(버스나 지하철 타기), getting off(내리기), transferring(갈아타기) 등의 표현을 정리했습니다. 안내 방송을 듣고 제대로 하차하기, interval(배차 간격), running hours(운행 시간)를 확인하는 표현도 함께 알아보겠습니다.

□ 여기서 동대문 시장까지 어떻게 가죠?	How do we go to the Dongdaemun Market?
□ 일단 마을버스를 타세요.	First, take a local bus. *local bus = town bus
□ 신촌 지하철역에서 하차하세요.	Get off at the Sinchon subway station.
□ 지하철 2호선을 타세요.	Take the subway Line No. 2.
□ 다음은 동대문역사문화공원역입니다.	The next station is Dongdaemun History & Culture Park station.
□ 환승역입니다.	It's the interchanges. *interchange = transfer station, junction
□ 4호선으로 갈아타세요.	Transfer to Line No. 4. *transfer = change
□ 동대문역까지 몇 정거장이죠?	How many stations to Dongdaemun station?
□ 몇 정거장이나 더 가야 하나요?	How many more stations (should we go)?
□ 한 정거장만 더 가면 됩니다.	Just one more station.
□ 지하철에서 내려서 6번 출구를 찾으세요.	Get off the subway, find the exit No.6.

□ 6번 출구로 나가세요.	Take the exit No. 6.
□ (시장에 가는) 다른 방법은 없나요?	Is there any other way (to get to the market)?
□ 노선 안내 방송을 잘 들으세요.	Pay attention to the route announcements.
□ 버스가 왜 이렇게 안 오지요?	Why isn't the bus coming? Why is the bus late?
□ 배차 간격이 몇 분인가요?	How often do they run? What's the interval between buses?
□ 5~8분 간격이에요.	They run every 5~8 minutes.
□ 들쑥날쑥 다녀요.	They run irregularly.
□ 첫차 시간이 언제입니까?	When is the first bus?
□ 막차 시간이 언제입니까?	When is the last bus?
□ 버스를 잘못 탔어요.	I've got on the wrong bus. I took the wrong bus.
□ 반대편에서 탔어야 했는데.	I should've taken the bus in the opposite side.
□ 버스를 놓쳤어요.	I missed the bus.
□ 서두르지 않으면 버스를 놓쳐요.	If you don't hurry up, you'll miss the bus.
□ (버스 기사의 말) 꼭 잡으세요.	Hold on tight, please.

📋 Notes

local bus 마을버스 junction 갈아타는 역, 환승역 route 노선, 루트 irregularly 불규칙적으로 hold on tight 단단히 붙들다, 꽉 잡다

04 택시 타기

택시를 타면 기사에게 원하는 길로 가 달라고 말하거나, 속도나 차내 온도 조절을 부탁하는 경우가 있죠. 또 원하는 장소에 내릴 때는 Pull over here, please.(여기서 세워 주세요.) 또는 Let/Drop me off at the crosswalk, please.(횡단보도에서 내려 주세요.)라고 하면 됩니다.

원어민 발음 듣기 ☑□   회화 훈련 □□   듣기 훈련 □□

□ 택시가 잘 안 잡히네요.	I can't get a cab.
□ 동대문 시장으로 가 주세요.	Take me to the Dongdaemun market, please.
	Go to the Dongdaemun market, please.
□ 어느 길로 갈까요?	Which route would you prefer? *route = way
□ 다니시던 길이 있나요?	Do you have usual route to go there?
□ 신촌 지하철역 쪽으로 가 주세요.	I'd like you to go through the Sinchon subway station.
□ 기사님이 알아서 가 주세요.	Take any route you like, please.
□ 지금 교통 체증이 없는 길을 아세요?	Do you know which road is open now?
□ 빨리 가 주세요.	Please hurry.
	Would you please speed up?
□ 너무 빨리 달리시네요.	You're driving too fast.
□ 속도를 늦춰 주세요.	Please slow down.
□ 아직인가요?	Are we there yet?
	How much further should we go?

▫ 거의 다 왔습니다.	We're almost there.
▫ 저기 횡단보도에서 내려 주세요.	Please let me off at the crossing. *let ~ off = drop ~ off *crossing = crosswalk
▫ 유턴해서 바로 세워 주세요.	Why don't you make a U-turn and pull over?
▫ 교차로 건너서 세워 주세요.	Cross the intersection and stop, please.
▫ 요금이 얼마죠?	What's the fare? How much do I owe you?
▫ 7,000원입니다.	It's 7,000 won.
▫ 카드로 계산할게요.	I'll pay by (credit) card.
▫ 기계에 카드를 대세요.	Put your card on the card machine.
▫ 영수증 주시겠어요?	Can I have the receipt?

📄 Notes

usual route 자주(늘) 가는 노선(길) speed up 속도를 높이다, 속도 내다 slow down 속도를 낮추다 let ~ off ~을 내려주다 pull over 차를 세우다, 멈추게 하다 fare 교통수단의 요금, 운임 owe 빚지다, 지불해야 하다

05 대중교통 티켓 요금

대중교통 요금은 흔히 fare라고 합니다. 한국 지하철의 경우 일회용 티켓 사용 후 내릴 때 ticket deposit(티켓 보증금)을 돌려받을 수 있습니다. 또한 한국과 미국 모두 일정 기간 동안 사용할 수 있는 metro card/pass(정기 승차권)가 있습니다.

원어민 발음 듣기 ☑□   회화 훈련 □□   듣기 훈련 □□

□ 지하철 요금은 얼마죠? — How much is the train fare?

□ 기본요금은 얼마죠? — How much is the basic fare?
*fare = charge

□ 일반 성인 요금은 얼마죠? — How much is the fare for general people?

□ 어린이 요금은 얼마죠? — How much is the children's fare?

□ 구간별로 다릅니다. — The fare depends on where you go.
It depends on how far you go.

□ 멀리 갈수록 요금이 추가됩니다. — The further you go, the more you have to pay.

□ 어디까지 가십니까? — Where is your destination?

□ 티켓 발매기를 이용하세요. — Please use the ticket machines.

□ 서울-부산 사이 KTX 요금은 얼마죠? — How much is the KTX train fare from Seoul to Pusan?

□ 5만 원 안팎입니다. — It's 50,000 won more or less.

□ 정기 승차권 주세요. — Metro pass, please.

📝 Notes

depend on ~에 달려 있다, ~에 따라 다르다   destination 목적지, 도착지   ticket machine 승차권, 티켓 판매기   more or less 대강, 대체로

06 면허 따기, 운전하기

MP3를 들어보세요 14-U06

운전을 능숙하게 잘 하는 사람을 good driver라고 합니다. 한편 driving/driver's test(운전면허 시험)을 준비할 때는 written test(필기시험)과 performance test(실기시험)의 시험 양식을 잘 파악해야 합니다.

원어민 발음 듣기 ☑□   회화 훈련 □□   듣기 훈련 □□

□ 자동차 면허는 땄어요?	Did you get your driver's license?
□ 장롱면허입니다.	I have a driver's license, but I don't drive.
□ 드라이브를 즐겨요.	I enjoy driving.
	I love to go for a ride.
□ 운전을 잘하시네요.	You're good at driving.
	You're a good driver.
	You drive well.
□ 길을 잘 아시네요.	You have a good sense of direction.
□ 운전을 잘 못해요.	I'm not a good driver.
□ 운전을 잘하고 싶어요.	I want to drive well.
□ 운전면허시험에서 또 떨어졌어요.	I failed my driving test again.
□ 운전면허시험을 한 번에 붙었어요.	I passed my driving test on the first try.
□ 운전을 잘하나요?	Do you drive well?
	Are you a good driver?
	Are you good at driving?
	*be good at = be good with
□ 나는 완전 초보 운전자야.	I'm a complete beginner.

□ 나는 10년 무사고 운전자야.	I've been driving my car for 10 years without a single accident.
	I have a perfect driving record for 10 years.
□ 운전 중엔 휴대폰을 사용하지 마.	Don't use your cell phone while driving.
□ 졸음운전은 금물이야.	Don't drive while you feel sleepy. *sleepy = drowsy
	Don't do sleepy driving.
	Don't be a sleepy driver.
□ 음주 운전은 금물이야.	Don't drink and drive.
□ 음주 운전은 매우 위험해.	It's very dangerous to drink and drive.
□ 운전면허를 취소당해.	Your driver's license will be revoked.
□ 음주 운전 단속 중이야.	There's a crackdown on drinking and driving. *crackdown = clampdown
□ 경찰관이 음주 측정기를 불라고 했어.	The policeman asked me to blow into the breathalyzer.

📝 Notes

go for a ride 드라이브 가다 a sense of direction 방향(길, 지리) 감각 get a lesson 수업(연수)받다 drowsy 졸리는, 식곤증 나는 drink and drive 음주 운전 하다 revoke 취소하다, 무효로 하다 crackdown 단속, 단속 조치(= clampdown) blow into ~에 입김을 불어넣다 breathalyzer 음주 측정기(= breath analyzer)

주유, 세차하기

MP3를 들어보세요 14-U07

"휘발유가 리터당 얼마입니까?"라고 물을 때는 How much is the gas/gasoline price per a liter?라고 합니다. 요즘은 알뜰한 운전자가 늘어서 직접 주유하는 self-service gas station(셀프 주유소)도 많아지고 있는 추세입니다.

원어민 발음 듣기 ☑□   회화 훈련 □□   듣기 훈련 □□

□ 이 근처에 주유소가 어디 있죠?	Where is the gas station near here?
□ 휘발유가 리터당 얼마죠?	How much is the gas price per a liter? *gas = gasoline
□ 리터당 2,000원입니다.	It's 2,000 won a liter.
□ 기름 값이 계속 오르고 있어요.	The gas prices are continuously increasing.
□ 기름 값이 계속 내리고 있어요.	The gas prices are continuously decreasing.
□ 주유소에 들릅시다.	Let's stop for gas at the (gas) station.
□ 차에 기름을 넣어야 해요.	We need to fill the fuel tank. We need to refuel.
□ 연료가 거의 바닥이에요.	The fuel tank is almost empty.
□ 10,000원어치 넣어 주세요.	Refuel 10,000 won, please. *refuel = fill
□ 가득 채워 주세요.	Fill her up. Tank up. Fill up the tank.

08 교통 법규

traffic laws(교통 법규)에 위반이 되는 행동으로는 speeding(과속), run(go through) a red light(신호 위반), ignoring the stop lines(정지선 무시) 등이 있습니다. 적발되면 traffic ticket(딱지)을 떼이고 fine/penalty(범칙금)를 내야 하죠. 특히 위반 사항이 심할 경우 운전자 penalty points(벌점)를 받을 수도 있습니다.

과속하셨습니다.	You were speeding.
신호를 위반하셨습니다.	You ran a red light. You went through a red light.
운전면허증, 차량 등록증을 제시하세요.	Can I see your driver's license and car registration? Your license and car registration, please.
딱지를 뗐어요.	I've got a traffic ticket. I was ticketed.
범칙금을 내야 해요.	I have to pay a fine. *fine = penalty
교통 신호를 잘 지키세요.	Pay attention to traffic signals. *signals = lights
정지선을 잘 보세요.	Don't violate the stop lines.
과태료 7만 원을 내야 돼요.	I have to pay 70,000 won for a fine.
벌점을 받았어요.	I received penalty points. *received = got
면허를 취소당했어요.	My driver's license was suspended. *suspended = revoked
항상 안전벨트를 매세요.	Keep your seat belt on.

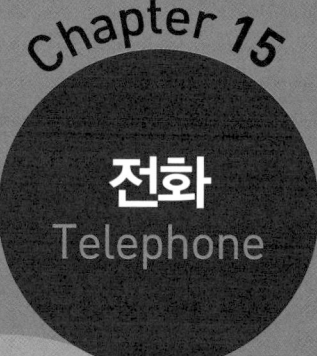

Chapter 15

전화
Telephone

01 전화 받기, 바꿔 주기   02 전화 걸기, 전화 끊기   03 메모 받기, 메모 남기기
04 용건 묻고 말하기   05 전화 상태, 통화 시 상황

01 전화 받기, 바꿔 주기

MP3를 들어보세요 15-U01

보통 Hello.(여보세요.), It's ~'s residence.(~네 집입니다.), It's ~'s cell phone.(~의 휴대폰입니다.)과 같이 전화 통화를 시작합니다. 다른 사람에게 전화를 바꿔 줄 때는 One moment, please.(잠시만요.)라고 말합니다.

원어민 발음 듣기 ☑☐   회화 훈련 ☐☐   듣기 훈련 ☐☐

☐ 전화벨이 울려.	The phone is ringing.
☐ 전화 안 받을 거야?	Aren't you going to answer that?
☐ 나 지금 전화 받을 수 없어.	I can't pick up the phone now.
☐ 대신 받아 줄래?	Would you pick it up for me?
☐ 나 찾으면 없다고 해.	Tell whoever it is, I'm not here.
☐ 메모만 받아 줄래?	Would you take a message for me?
☐ 다시 건다고 말해 줄래?	Tell her I'll call back. Would you tell him that I'll call back?
☐ 여보세요.	Hello.
☐ 김 씨네 집입니다.	(This is) Kim's residence.
☐ 크리스털 휴대폰입니다.	(It's) Crystal's cell phone.
☐ 제가 크리스털인데요.	It's Crystal. Crystal speaking. This is she (speaking).
☐ 예, 바꿔드릴게요.	Sure. I'll get her for you.
☐ 예, 잠시만요.	Sure. One moment, please.
☐ 크리스털, 네 전화야.	Crystal, it's for you.

☐ 다급한 목소리야.	She sounds urgent.
☐ 나 좀 바꿔 줘.	Let me talk to her.
☐ 그는 잠깐 외출했어요.	He is out for a minute.
☐ 그는 통화 중이에요.	His phone line is busy.
☐ 그는 잠시 자리를 비웠어요.	He is not into the office right now.
	He is out of the office right now.
☐ 금방 돌아올 거예요.	She will be back soon.
☐ 그는 휴가 중입니다.	He is on his vacation.
	*vacation = holiday
	He is away on leave.
	He has been off work.
☐ 누구시죠?	Who's speaking?
	Who's calling?
	May I ask who this is?
	Who is this?
☐ N 사입니다. 무엇을 도와드릴까요?	N Company. What can I help you?
	N Company. How may I help you?

Notes

organic 무공해 유기농법의, 유기농 식품의   treats 간식   jerky 말린 고기, 육포
supplement 보조 식품, 영양제   live on ~을 먹고 살다, ~을 주식으로 하다   seed 씨, 씨앗
worm (지렁이, 구더기 등의) 벌레

02 전화 걸기, 전화 끊기

전화를 걸 때 "~와 통화하고 싶은데요."는 I'd like to talk to ~. 또는 Can I speak to ~?라고 표현합니다. 찾는 사람이 자신이 맞다면 This is she/he (speaking).라고 하면 됩니다. 전화를 끊을 때도 I gotta go.(끊어야겠다.), I'm hang up.(끊을게.) 등 여러 가지 표현이 있습니다.

원어민 발음 듣기 ☑☐   회화 훈련 ☐☐   듣기 훈련 ☐☐

☐ 크리스털과 통화하고 싶은데요.	I'd like to talk to Crystal. *talk = speak Can I talk to Crystal?
☐ 잠깐만. 다른 전화가 왔어.	Hold on a second. I've got another call. Hold on. I've got someone on another line. Hold on. I have a call on the other line.
☐ 끊지 마.	Don't hang up.
☐ 수 전화번호 좀 알려 줘.	Let me have Sue's phone number. Can I have Sue's number? Do you know Sue's number?
☐ 전화번호가 있는지 잘 모르겠어.	I'm not sure that I have her number. I'm not sure whether I have it.
☐ 전화번호부 좀 확인할게.	I'll check my phone book. Let me check my phone book.
☐ 그만 끊어야겠다.	I gotta go. I've got to go. Let's hang up.

□ 자주 좀 전화해.	Call me more often. *call=ring
□ 내일 전화할게.	I'll call you tomorrow.
□ 도착하자마자 전화할게.	I'll call you as soon as I arrive.
□ 언제 통화할 수 있어?	When can I call you? When can I talk to you on the phone? When are you available to talk?
□ 시간 나면 전화해.	Call me when you have time. *when=if Give me a call whenever you have time.
□ 전화 끊을게.	I'm going to hang up. I'm hanging up.
□ 네가 먼저 끊어.	You hang up first.
□ 안녕. 들어가.	Bye.

  Notes

hang up 수화기를 놓다, 전화를 끊다   **gotta** ~해야 한다(=have got to)   **have time** 시간 나다, 여유가 생기다

03 메모 받기, 메모 남기기

MP3를 들어보세요 15-U03

전화로 메모를 받을 때는 Can I take a message?(메모를 남겨 드릴까요?), 메모를 남기고 싶을 때는 Could you leave a message for me?(메모를 남겨 주시겠어요?)라고 말하면 됩니다. 보통 메모 내용은 전화 건 사람의 이름과 연락처, 걸려온 시간 등과 같은 간단한 사항입니다.

원어민 발음 듣기 ☑□   회화 훈련 □□   듣기 훈련 □□

□ 메모를 남겨 드릴까요?	Can I take a message? Do you want to leave a message? Do you want me to take a message for you?
□ 예, 그래 주시면 감사하겠습니다.	Yes, I'd appreciate if you do that. Yes, it would be appreciated.
□ 성함이 어떻게 되시죠?	May I have your name? Can I have your full name, please?
□ 이름 철자를 불러 주세요.	Could you spell your name, please?
□ 성은 어떻게 되시죠?	What's your last name? May I ask what your last name is? *may = can
□ 제 성은 김입니다.	My last name is Kim. It's Kim.
□ 연락처는 어떻게 되시죠?	What's your phone number? *phone = contact Can I have your phone number? Your phone number, please.
□ 그가 당신 연락처를 알고 있나요?	Does he know your phone number? How can he reach you?

	What number can he call?
☐ 휴대폰 번호를 알려 드릴게요.	I'll give you my cell number.
☐ 이 번호로 전화 주시면 됩니다.	You can contact me at this number.
	Call this number.
☐ 그녀에게 전화하라고 할까요?	Shall I have her call you?
	Do you want me to have her call you back?
☐ 전화하라고 전할게요.	I'll tell her to call you back.
☐ 제가 몇 시쯤 전화하면 될까요?	When should I call her?
☐ 메모를 남겨 주시겠어요?	Could you leave a message for me?
☐ 전화했었다고 전해 주세요.	Tell him that I called.
	Would you please tell him that I called?
☐ 전화 기다린다고 전해 주세요.	Tell her that I'll be waiting for her returning call.
	Please tell her that I'll be expecting her call.
☐ 급한 일이라고 전해 주세요.	Tell him that it's urgent.
	Tell him that it's an urgent matter.
☐ 그가 방금 전화했었어요.	He just called.

04 용건 묻고 말하기

MP3를 들어보세요 15-U04

전화 건 사람의 용건을 물을 때는 친한 사이가 아닌 이상 예의 있게 May I ask what this is about?(무슨 일인지 여쭤봐도 될까요?)라고 하면 됩니다. 대답할 때는 I'm calling (you) about ~.(~때문에 전화했어요.)라고 합니다. 전화상에서 용건을 묻고 대답하는 표현을 살펴보겠습니다.

원어민 발음 듣기 ☑☐   회화 훈련 ☐☐   듣기 훈련 ☐☐

□ 잠시 통화 괜찮으세요?   Do you have a moment?
                                        Can I talk to you for a second?

□ 무슨 용건이시죠?   May I ask what this is about?
                                        What is this about?

□ (친한 사이에) 무슨 일이야?   What's up?

□ 무슨 일 있어?   What's going on?
                                        What's wrong?

□ 궁금한 것이 있어서 전화했어.   I'm calling because I want to ask you (about) something.

□ 중요한 용건이 있어서 전화했어.   I'm calling because I have an important thing to say.

□ 급한 일이라서 전화했어.   I'm calling because it's urgent.

□ 그것 때문에 전화한 거야?   Are you calling me because of that?

□ 전화 기다리고 있었어.   I've been waiting for your call.
                                        I'm expecting you to call.
                                        I was anticipating your call.

□ 메모 받자마자 전화했어요.   I'm calling you as soon as I got your message.

□ 전에 전화드렸던 크리스털입니다.   This is Crystal. I called you a couple of days ago.

05 전화 상태, 통화 시 상황

전화 통화를 할 때에는 잡음이 심하거나, 주위가 시끄럽거나, 양손에 물건이 있는 등 여러 가지 상황이 있을 수 있습니다. 그러니 통화가 연결되자마자 Is it okay to talk now?(지금 통화 괜찮아?)라며 상대편에게 전화를 받아도 괜찮은 상황인지를 먼저 묻는 것이 좋겠죠.

원어민 발음 듣기 ☑□   회화 훈련 □□   듣기 훈련 □□

소리가 (전혀) 안 들려요.	I can't hear you (at all).
좀 더 크게 말씀해 주시겠어요?	Can you speak up? Speak loudly, please.
듣고 있어요?	Are you (still) there?
잡음이 심해요.	There's lots of static on the line. My phone has lots of static.
주변 소음이 심해요.	It's too noisy around you. There's too much noise out there.
전화가 갑자기 끊겼어요.	The phone was suddenly cut off. The phone was suddenly disconnected. I was suddenly cut off. *was=got The line went dead suddenly.
배터리가 다 됐어요.	My phone battery is dead. The battery has run down.
전화기가 곧 꺼질 거예요.	My phone will be dead soon.
전화기가 꺼져 있어요.	My phone has gone dead. My phone is turned off. Is this a bad time to talk?

지금 전화하기 곤란해.	I can't talk to you right now. This is not a good time to talk.
전화로 말하긴 좀 그렇다.	I can't talk to you about this on the phone.
나 지금 뭐 좀 하는 중이야.	I'm in the middle of something.
저 지금 회의 중인데요.	I'm in the meeting.
저 누구와 면담 중인데요.	I'm talking with someone. I'm having a meeting with someone.
나중에 내가 다시 걸게.	Can I call you back later? Let me call you again.
내가 다시 걸까?	Do you want me to call back? Should I call you back later?
바로 다시 걸게.	I'll call you back right away.
그가 전화를 안 받아.	He won't pick up the phone. He doesn't answer the phone.

Notes

speak up 큰 소리로 말하다 static 전파 장애 cut off 자르다, 절단하다, 끊다 go dead 죽어가다, 죽다, 꺼지다 in the middle of 한창 ~하는 중인